WHO'S WALLY?

Adoption, Brian, and Me.

By

Andy Wallis

Inspired by the blog

www.whoswally.co.uk

For David.

Contents (of my head)

Dear Wally,

I can't put into words how proud I am of you right now Andy, it makes me very emotional to see this new positivity in you. Your writing is heartfelt and honest with your own touch of humour, it's brilliant. I hope that by writing this book you are able to help other adoptees, partners, and families of adoptees as much as helping yourself. I cannot wait to have a copy of your book in print.

I am well aware that the road we are now on is not going to be an easy one, there is a lot to learn and discover, and I have no idea where it will lead us, but I want to share this journey with you, support and help you as much as I can.

I see you now and I believe we are worth it.

Em x

The Missing Allen Key

I'm not a celebrity, a politician, a football manager, a reformed master criminal, or famous for being on 'Big Brother'. I'm not writing these words to massage my ego, crack the USA, or make you, the reader like me. I'm not even doing it to sell this book (although that seems quite counter-productive now I consider the amount of effort it's taken).

So, why would anyone bother to read this book?

That's a good question.

I'm assuming that you are bothering to, otherwise, how would you be reading this? Have you bought it? If so, thank you. Alternatively, if you are just killing time standing in a bookshop waiting for the rain to pass then you may as well buy it. You know, in the way you might feel obliged to order a quick drink when you pop into a pub, just to use the toilet.

I'm writing these words to help myself. I need to know me. The *real* me, not the pretend me that so often, is the first person you speak to when you meet me, or at least that's how it feels.

The *real* me never feels part of a group, the *real* me refuses to let people in and runs away, the *real* me feels like a fraud in almost every situation, and breaks his back to help people or say the right thing just to feel acceptance. Like me, like me, LIKE ME!

The *real* me gets depressed and suffers weird moments of anxiety and hates letting go of the gorilla grip he has on life for fear of losing control. I often feel trapped inside myself, holding myself back and that feeling is almost comforting. Like I'm at a funeral and I can't be seen to be happy for the sake of the other mourners. There's much more that I'll hopefully learn as I write.

I'm adopted. There, I said it!

After a year of some dark and miserable times, I thought "Wally, enough is enough, this has gone on too long". I've not thought about being adopted much, it's just something that happened to that child fifty years ago that I feel no connection to, I was wrong.

Although I feel very little connection with 'David' (my birth name), he still plays a very big part in my thinking and decision-making, so I started to look deeper into myself and the effects that adoption has on my tiny adoptee's brain. The more I discovered about adoption and its 'trauma', the more I saw it in me.

As I start to write this book it is already giving me issues. Will I have enough to write a book, or will I just run out of things to say? How much is relevant? What shouldn't I include? Then, what should I do with it, publish it, blog it? And most importantly, can I be honest enough? If you have followed any of my journey online, then you will already be aware that I run the 'Who's Wally?' blog. One thing is for sure, there is very little honest and open 'first-person experience' stuff written by adopted men, especially in the UK.

I have nothing to lose and possibly lots to gain, including my sanity, well what's left of it.

If sanity was an Ikea Billy bookcase, then I've got the Allen key missing.

What was the question again? Oh yes, why bother reading the book? Firstly, two pairs of eyes are better than one and without that Allen key, we can't build the bookcase, and you will need somewhere to put the book. Secondly, and probably more importantly, writing is teaching me a lot about myself, and there's a chance that if you are an adoptee, a partner, friend, or family member of an adoptee, you might pick up a thing or two as well. Who knows.

Also, just so you know, the only real names that will appear on the pages of Who's Wally? are mine,

Andy Wallis (Birth name David Rice), my partner, Em Bacon, oh and there's a certain 'Brian' that gets a mention here and there. All other people referenced along the way have had their real names changed.

Wally 101

My name has been Andrew Philip Charles Wallis for most of my life (yeah, I know), but when I was born I was a Dave, David Charles Rice to be exact.

David was surplus to requirements. Andrew, on the other hand, was "chosen". David was given up for adoption by the woman who carried him for nine months, then "chosen" by people who couldn't have children and had a 'David' sized hole in their lives. Hey, I'm a 'David', I'd fit perfectly in there! And I did.

Three years after I was adopted, my adopted sister came along and we were living in Sawley, in Derbyshire, it wasn't the rural village you're thinking of, it was a large housing estate near Junction 24 of the M1. I have very little memory of living there,

I remember the street and what the house looked like, and the street party we had for the Queen's Silver Jubilee in 1977.

We weren't living there very long before my parents decided to move, so my sister and I did most of our growing up in a small place called Toton in Nottingham. The name Toton might be familiar to some as it is one of the places the new High-Speed Rail Network (HS2) will have a Parkway to serve Nottingham and Derby. Toton is a bit of a strange place, I'm not even sure what to call it, it's not small or quaint enough to be a village, nor is it right to call it a town as it doesn't have a centre of shops. It sits in the middle between Stapleford, Long Eaton, and Beeston, all of which have shopping areas. Toton is, in my opinion at least, a housing estate that just got a bit too big. Of course, it has the huge obligatory Tesco, and a handful of corner shops dotted around, but that's about it.

We moved in 1979 into a three-bedroom detached house that was just two doors away from our Grandparents (Dad's parents). We lived with them for a while so that they could do up the house a bit before we moved in.

Dad spent most of his working life as a storekeeper at a power station until the station closed in the late eighties and he was made redundant. He went on to study Theology for a year and both he and Mum are now involved with a church nearby and they love it. Later Dad worked as a day care worker looking after disabled adults and he really enjoyed his time there.

Mum gave up her job as a clerical worker at an army barracks (where they both met as Dad worked there too for a while) to have us kids. Later when we were a few years older, she was an 'out worker' for a local telecommunications company. She would walk four miles with my sister and me to collect heavy hand presses, then walk us all back. She would then take deliveries of boxes of plastic parts to press together at home. Looking back, she was pretty amazing, she was the one who kept it all together, running the house, sorting out us kids, and still working from home at the same time. In the late eighties/early nineties, Mum worked as chief cashier at various big stores, looking after the money and balancing their books. Then, after our Gran died in 1995 she stopped working to become Grandad's carer as he had suffered strokes in later life.

Gran and Grandad were a big part of our childhood. We would see them almost daily and spent a lot of time with them, especially later during school holidays. Often Gran's would be the place I would go if I got really dirty when I was out playing. I'd be worried that I'd be told off by Mum, so Gran would clean me up before I went home. Gran would always give me money for petrol when I first started driving and let me have cigarettes when I ran out. It took me a long time to grieve after their deaths, I still miss them. I think about them every time I drive past the house.

Nana, we pronounced it '*Nannar*' was Mum's Mum. I wish I could recall more of her. I never knew my Grandad from Mum's side as he died before I was born and sadly Nana died when she was just fifty-nine, after suffering from dementia. I remember her little terraced house, stuck in the 1950's that always seemed cold. Even though it must be forty years since I've been there, I can still walk around the house in my mind and recall the smells and how the light fell into the rooms.

We had a typical upbringing I think, we both went to schools very close to home. We had pets, a rabbit, guinea pigs, and hamsters. Once we had a few chickens, I'm not sure why. They were noisy and smelly and were ultimately given to a gamekeeper friend of Dad's, who ate them. I don't think I really cared for any of the pets we had, Dad tells me the rabbit was given to a school and it was three weeks before I realised it had gone. Is that like when kids are told that the family dog went to 'live on a farm' when really it's dead? I'm fifty Dad, if the rabbit died, you can tell me.

In the seventies we spent a lot of time on the east coast around Skegness, we mostly stayed in static caravans on a site called Golden Sands in Ingoldmells. I can still picture the Bingo halls and arcades. I drove through recently, it's so different now, I didn't recognise a thing which made me feel a little sad.

In the eighties we holidayed abroad, often taking two-day coach trips to Spain or Italy. We were almost driven off a cliff edge when the driver fell asleep on one of the trips. Let me tell you, nobody was settled enough to have an afternoon snooze after that!

Our parents were, and still are there for us, backing my sister and I up at every turn and helping us out of the sticky spots we find ourselves in. I love my parents very much, I am truly thankful for them and their sacrifices for both me and my sister over the years. I've lost count of how many times I've moved back home after a break-up, needed money, or just needed someone to talk to without fear of being judged. I know that adoptees are often called 'special' and 'chosen', but those labels have not served me well over the years, but what I do feel is very lucky, after being born into a family that didn't want me. Then having the chance of a family that did, life could have been very different.

Growing up in our family home was great mostly. I always felt comfortable, loved, and cared for, except for when I did something I shouldn't have, it was the seventies and eighties, and kids were put in their place properly back then! I was never that academic growing up and consequently would spend what felt like hours going through maths textbooks with Dad over the kitchen table. It just didn't seem to sink in. I remember often being in tears as Dad tried his best to explain things that were just bouncing off me.

I could accept that 10x10=100. But why does it? How far back into the theory did I need to go? It's 100, it just is, but just knowing the answer wasn't enough. Did I really need a '10s' origin story? Talking later with my fifteen-year-old daughter who also openly admits that maths isn't her strongest subject, I discovered that she also struggles with the same issue. Yes, you can do the sum. Yes, it adds up. But why does it? I was so concerned with 'why' I lost sight of 'what'.

Home life and maths aside, being independent has been more difficult. Since moving out of the family home, I've never felt truly at home anywhere, no matter how long I've stayed in one place, or with whom. I'm always on a knife edge.

Not necessarily anxious all the time, but absolutely on the brink of anxiousness. I've never felt settled. I've been living unsettled in this house now since 2018, and although I enjoy coming 'home' and I look after it as best I can, it is a rented property, so perhaps that has something to do with the feeling. But even when I have owned houses in the past, there was always something a miss.

When you hear the word 'adoption' what do you think of? I bet it's images of a loving couple getting the chance to love a child that nature had cruelly decided they couldn't make for themselves, right? Well, if you are reading this and you're *not* an adoptee then you could well be thinking that, and that's ok. But if you are on the other side of the adoption fence, then things aren't always as green on that grass.

Finding a forever family for an otherwise unwanted child is amazing, isn't it?

I've spoken to my parents about their experiences of adopting my sister and me and they had nothing but good things to tell me. We were adopted as babies, both just a few months old, and according to them, we settled in well and were as perfect to them as babies get.

No doubt they could have done with being woken less at night and for us to come fitted with volume control, but on the whole, normal and lovely to them.

There was a short period when I was nearly six months old when my birth mother may have wanted me back, as it was thought that she wouldn't be able to have any more children. That didn't happen in the end, so all was well for the Wallis family.

Both my sister and I were blonde and blue-eyed as kids, as is our adoptive Mum. It was often commented that there was quite a family resemblance, that usually came with an element of surprise after people found out we were adopted.

I have always known I was adopted, at least I can't recall being told, and I also believed that I haven't been affected by my adoption. I mean I know I have my issues and after having a few different sessions with counsellors over the last ten years, you would be forgiven for thinking that I was at peace with who I am. Well, no. I'm still none the wiser. This year, 2023, I had an almighty crash landing, falling into a black hole I couldn't escape.

I had shut the world out and the door was LOCKED!

As I've said, the 'Chosen' thing, sometimes coupled with the word 'Special' are words that adoptees often hate, as it sets them apart from the rest of the world right from the start. It sounds lovely to be 'chosen' and 'special' doesn't it? Who wouldn't want to be that? I can see why adopters might have been advised to say these things to their child. Perhaps they were informed that it could help the child feel wanted, and loved, or help them settle into their new family.

In reality, I fear it might make children feel different, not part of the group, and possibly feel like an outsider in their own lives.

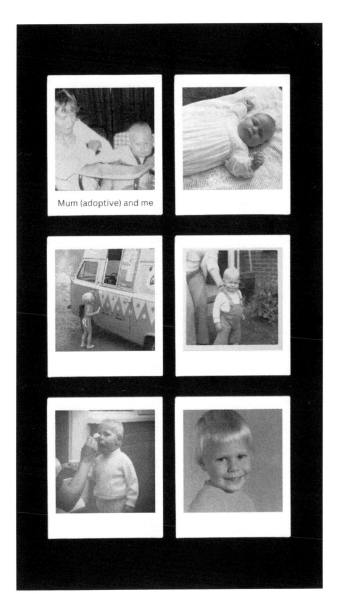

Mum (adoptive) and me

Em Looks From The Outside In

I was being pushed away. Andy had cemented that last brick in the wall he had been building between us over the last year.

That metaphorical wall had been cemented using a mixture of emotions, destructive self-beliefs, depression, and anxiety.

I was a mess; this was not what I wanted or what I truly believed Andy wanted either. There was more to this, I was sure. I just had to find out what it was.

We met at a time when we were both going through a lonely period in our lives, so it felt amazing to find each other and feel alive again. We just clicked, such a cliché but I can't say it any other way. Talking every day, being open and honest, sharing music, laughing about the same stupid stuff, and just enjoying being in each other's company. Also, it totally helps when that chemical reaction happens, and you can't keep your hands off someone!

Speaking about our pasts, Andy told me from the get-go that he was adopted and was very blasé about it. It never seemed to be something that he had any problems with or even thought about. Quite early on we found out we both, like a lot of people, suffer from a lack of self-esteem, overthink, and over analyse. Both admitted to experiencing bouts of depression and that he had tried counselling before. I did at this time, mention whether his adoption had anything to do with it, but he just shrugged it off. I look back on that conversation now and see it very differently.

We fell 'in love'. It was a romantic, beautiful relationship, not just in a physical or conversational way, but emotionally too. Sharing our inner thoughts and feelings and wanting to help and support each other. Andy made me feel so loved and wanted, and I wanted him to feel that from me too.

Being the kind, generous, clever, (Andy never believed me when I said this to him) and practical person he is, I would get flowers every time we saw each other, he would travel miles (we live 94 miles from each other) to help me and my family, buy little things I may need, even make me tools I could use for my work. Don't get me wrong it was so lovely to have someone I loved, do these things, but I did recognise then, that this was a people-pleasing trait and felt at times it wasn't necessary.

He didn't need to win my love, I was all in. We were 'Us'.

I thought it came from a lack of self-esteem, which we had discussed before. But as time went on, I realised it was way deeper than that.

Our social lives were quite different, I came from a very sociable background with many friends. Whereas, at the time, Andy lived a quiet and quite solitary lifestyle, apart from work, a few friends, kids, and his family. This I now know, is due to Andy keeping his world small, comfortable, and anxiety-free.

Due to us not living near each other, our day-to-day relationship was mainly conducted through messages and video calls. We would travel to see each other and our families when we could (which wasn't often enough, to be honest). Most of the time this was great, and it worked. But long-distance relationships are not easy, especially when both parties have a tendency to over analyse, and take things personally by reading totally different intentions in a text message.

We would have bouts where we would miss each other terribly and try to work out how we could fix the problem, but we both had our own kids' lives to consider, so just packing up and moving in together wasn't an option. But we always managed to get back to being happy, we had each other and enjoyed what we had.

But then there were the times when his tone of voice would change, there was an underlying anger, a hint of jealousy, and just being a bit of an arse. I knew deep down that this just wasn't Andy. This would usually happen when I was doing something with a group of friends, going somewhere for the weekend, or not replying to a message straight away. I would get short messages, or none at all. If I did get replies, they just sounded off. Basically, pushing me away. This would then play havoc with my insecurities and made me feel as if I was doing something wrong. So, instead of me enjoying my time, I would be thinking about us and what it all meant, trying to understand the situation.

"How can he be like this, he knows I love him", and making me feel hurt and sad. It even made me question if I was in a toxic manipulative relationship!

This would then lead to conversations about how my life was so different, why would I want to be with someone who didn't like to go to parties, or be in large groups of people, I'd be better off without him stopping me from doing things. To me, this didn't make sense as I have seen a charismatic, funny guy who can hold his own in a group of people! No matter what I said, he never felt he would fit in or be good enough.

This I now know is the beginning of an anxiety episode, where a minor thought in his head will spiral out of control, and become so intensely overwhelming mentally and physically that he can't think rationally.

That reminds me of the first time Andy had a full-on anxiety attack in my company.

We were camping with my friends, there was loud dance music and people partying. We'd been drinking most of the day, but then something changed and he walked off, broke down, and started being sick. I didn't understand what was happening. I just thought he'd had too much to drink, so I managed to get him to bed (well, into a tent). I fully admit I wasn't the most supportive girlfriend that night, I was a bit pissed off if I'm honest. The next day was difficult, he was super quiet and kept wandering off for hours so I didn't know where or how he was. I just wanted him to talk to me. Looking back on that now, I had no idea the struggle he was going through with his thoughts. If I had known what I know now, I would have dealt with it in such a different way. I get very emotional thinking about that time and wish I had been able to help.

After any anxious thoughts, among other things, he would tell me he wasn't good enough, and I'd be better off without him. We would have conversations for days, ending up with one-word replies, and then eventually becoming almost silent. I would be left feeling empty and making up all sorts of scenarios of where he was and what he was doing and with whom. Pushing me away to a point where he thought I would eventually say goodbye. Building a wall between us, that neither of us could break through.

But I would always give him a bit of time, as I thought this was Andy suffering from depression, and he would find his way out of it, plus I felt it wasn't the 'real him' that was saying these things. This happened a couple of times, and we sort of got back on track, chatting, and seeing each other again but it never felt like he was fully back with me.

The thing is, I loved Andy with all my heart, so how could I let go of him?

Throughout this time, I had said maybe he should write down everything that he was thinking, so I bought him a pad and some pencils.

I knew Andy had always sketched and made notes and did a bit of writing, but I wanted to encourage it. Plus, his messages to me were always so open and honest, and articulate, I thought he would be good at it. I also thought it would be a great help to sort out what was going on in his head.

I hated what was happening between us. His mood swings were affecting me, and my busy life obviously caused him some anxiety. I did question what I was doing in this relationship, and how it was making me feel. So, with my mind going bananas about being in a manipulative toxic relationship, I Googled it, of course. I don't think I actually believed it was that kind of relationship, but I needed to get underneath it all, there was something not right here.

I just had an urge to understand what was going on, and why he thought the way he did.

So many aspects were not relevant, but a few things that cropped up while I was searching were 'lack of self-esteem', 'trauma', and 'fear of abandonment'. This then led me to research 'Adoption Trauma'. So glad I did, it shouted out from the page. Was this what was going on? I had to find out more. Little did I know what it all meant then though.

In April, after another bout of depression and endless conversations, I knew he was in a bad way, knew he wasn't eating properly, barely surviving, just managing to get to work, but that was it. This man meant so much to me, I had to see him, and I needed to make sure he was ok. I decided to visit, I got in my car the next day and drove ninety-four miles.

On that journey, I listened to a book entitled 'Adoption Trauma' by Fiona Myles. I couldn't believe what I was hearing, so many aspects of her life as an adoptee rang true to how he came across to me. It made me realise there were explanations for his behaviour and how he dealt with situations, and more importantly how he felt about himself. It was like she was talking about Andy.

When I got there, he was a shell of the person I knew, frail, physically and mentally. It scared me to see Andy like that. I knew he didn't like me seeing him that way, I could tell he was anxious. So, we had a coffee, and I managed to get him out for a walk. Later in the day, I mentioned that I had listened to an audiobook that I think he would find interesting. I wasn't sure how it would go down, but what did I have to lose?

I went home the next day, glad to have seen him, but I was worried.

The next day I got a message that he had listened to the book. I was amazed, I didn't expect him to have done that so quickly. He also found it enlightening, as if it was all about him and it started a new thought process within. He recognised so many traits. I couldn't believe what he was telling me, it seemed to flick a switch on in his head. I also sent Andy the link to' Primal Wound' by Nancy Verrier. I'd read that it is a renowned book that seems to be revered by all parties in the adoption process. He bought it and started to read it. Religiously.

Over the next few weeks, it became apparent to us both that adoption trauma is a thing and that it's within him. Anne Heffron's book 'You Don't Look Adopted' was the next book I listened to, I felt he definitely should read this too.

Since then, we have had our ups and downs, and our time apart as he started to come out of the fog, and understand what he was learning about himself. So, that's when he started to write everything down.

That was the wonderful beginning of 'Who's Wally?'

The writing is helping him to embrace the journey of finding out who he is and understand more about Adoption Trauma. He has completed a college course on understanding Mental Health As well as started personal counselling. As I'm sure he would tell you, failure is not an option for Andy.

Em and me.

Brian

In Phil Stutz's book 'The Tools'[1], he refers to the negative, dark part of a person's mind as their "shadow". I call mine "Brian" as opposed to 'brain'. Calling him Brian was Em's idea. She often called the brain Brian to amuse herself and has often asked me "How is Brian?" I liked it, so it has stuck. It's good to give my issues a name, it makes them sound small, less dominating, almost silly and it puts them in their place. Yes they are there, but they are not Andy, they are Brian, and he is a twat.

How much of twat? Imagine a small annoying little man, in a brown smock coat.

---

[1] The Tools was written by Phil Stutz and Barry Michels and they have been Referred to as "the most sought-after shrinks in Hollywood"

A sort of, bitter, tight-fisted shopkeeper with a somewhat mono-toned delivery to his voice, soaking up the joy and positivity from the floor of any situation, with his squeegee mop and bucket of doom, he takes great pleasure in it too. He is not required in any situation, but often his presence is a comfort. Brian has been there a long time and although I've been more aware of him in the last ten years, it's only recently that I've started to believe that he's been around since birth. I'm one of the children that was a problem before I was born. Once that problem was 'removed' by being relinquished, Brian saw a gap in the market, bought the plot, drew his plans, and unbeknown to me, began building.

Was Brian building from foundations of relinquishment? Were my attachment issues born in my mind just after I was? Maybe. It's a theory and it is the whole reason for this book. I see myself in other adoptees' experiences, and I have the feeling

Brian's wiring is related. Brian will crop up now and again, keep an eye out for the irritating little shit!

Who's Wally? Becomes a Thing

I started at the beginning, literally the first chapter. I've written a lot over the years from blogs to technical and photography manuals[2], But when it came to putting a book together, you may as well have asked me to juggle chainsaws on a unicycle[3].

You see, I have started books before, three or four chapters of each, at best. I'd have a great idea, start frantically writing, then run out of enthusiasm leaving them unfinished. These little bits of writing just sat in my online cloud account, ending up on every computer I've owned since. Like that box of belongings, you move from house to house only to then put it in the loft and never open it.

---

[2] I spent twenty years working for a packaging machinery company.
[3] I can't do that by the way, that was the point you see. No circus training whatsoever.

These unfinished 'masterpieces' are taunting me, reminding me of my severe lack of commitment, while singing "Pro-crastinater" to the tune of Smooth Operator by Sade. I know you're singing it in your head now. If you're on the bus reading this, sing it out loud … go on, I dare you.

This time, however, I just couldn't stop, I'd sit in front of my laptop, and after thirty minutes of; Type. Delete. Think. Type. Repeat, I was off, falling over my fingers to get it down as fast as possible. Full of typos and grammatical errors (so many red lines!) but I didn't care. It was pouring out. Not to mention the huge surge of enthusiasm I had for the newfound authorship.

Two weeks in, seven thousand words later and I was starting to feel the pressure of a book. That weight made me panic a little, and as soon as I began, I found myself slowing down. Could I really be peaking so soon?

The point of writing was to understand myself more, and that wasn't going to happen if I couldn't get the words out of my mind and onto the screen. I needed to change the way I was doing this.

A blog maybe? Writing articles instead of chapters I could explore my mind in smaller chunks. I'd used Blogger before which I kind of understood, meaning I could spend less time learning and more time writing. And … It's free.

June the 17th, 2023, Who's Wally? *The blog* received its first post. Shit! I was nervous. Writing about my inner self was hard enough, but posting it online was another matter entirely!

Sharing online, albeit to nobody, meant releasing some of the gorilla grip I had on life and it was not a pleasant experience.

Nevertheless, I was facing it with newfound confidence.

Or was I?

Oh, I don't know! Maybe.

What the hell are you doing Wally?

I didn't do social media, the less I was out there, the more control I had. Late one night, I logged onto Facebook and searched for a group I'd read about in the book by Fiona Myles, mentioned previously by Em. The group was called 'This is me - I'm adopted' and was for adult adoptees. Having found the group, I clicked to join and then went to bed.

The following morning I saw that my application had been declined. Had I broken the group rules already? This set my anxiety off on its shit-shaped rocket. After a few days of thinking about it, I crumbled and emailed Fiona to the address that I found on her website.

I felt a bit overfamiliar doing it, and that too made me feel quite uncomfortable. Within five minutes she had replied with an apology saying that the group rules weren't satisfied. No profile image. Phew! That was all it was, but now I had to put my face online, I didn't like that idea at all.

I opted for an image taken of me and my eleven-year-old son, we were both standing on molehills in a field, it was in black and white, and more importantly we were facing away from the camera. I checked back to find my introduction message had now appeared at the top of the group field. The message read;

"*Hello. New.*

I was adopted in 1973. Really struggled with social and relationships. Finally facing it and recognising it. Only took fifty years!

I also have issues with social media, finding that I struggle with letting go of control and end up with huge anxieties over it, so this is a big leap for me. I can't even bring myself to add a photo these days ... We'll see."

I was using the blog as a place to write without the pressure, it was going well but, I started to consider that it might help someone else. It was relatively safe so far, tucked away in my little HTML cupboard under Tim Berners-Lee's[4] 'digital stairwell'. However, helping others couldn't happen if I didn't share it.

I was shaking, actually shaking, as I sent that first post to that Facebook group, I almost completed the job peering through my fingers. But I'd done it!

It got a few 'likes' and some nice comments of encouragement. so I considered that a success.

---

[4] Tim Berners-Lee invented the World Wide Web in 1989

Now I felt I'd started to recognise my adoption and its effect on my life. Moreover, there are others out there feeling the same.

I couldn't get rid of the shakes for days afterward. I felt extremely vulnerable, even more than usual! But I persevered and kept posting. "I'm heading in the right direction." I might have said out loud. I mean, I could have made that up, I might have sat in silence and not even thought about it. But for dramatic effect, I said it out loud. OK? [Sticks out tongue, in a really childish way]

Since then the blog has grown, and Who's Wally? is now a thing. It has its own proper URL **www.whoswally.co.uk** and in the first six weeks of its existence, it attracted over three thousand, five hundred visitors.

People have found it resonates with something in their lives and have commented, 'liked', and shared its relevance to them.

It has even attracted guest bloggers. All the folks involved in whatever way they chose have made me feel part of a community that I previously thought didn't exist.

I have more determination to write and explore now, and I feel as if I am writing for more than just myself. For that, I am extremely grateful.

I Need To Know - *Part One*

I have very little knowledge of my beginnings. Just a couple of months old when I was transferred to my 'forever family', so there are key sections of first-hand information missing, in my adopted family memories. I'm sure to them it doesn't seem like a big deal, for me though, and no doubt for many others in my position it feels weird. We can't ask our adopted parents what our birth was like or how they felt carrying us for nine months, can we? And what about that medical history question at the doctor's surgery? "Sorry Doctor, I was adopted, I've no idea if there's a family history of piles". "Why are you putting on gloves? It's the middle of June and quite warm in here!"

I'd say that I wasn't interested in finding out more about my adoption. But the more grey hair[5] I acquired the more I wanted to know.

---

[5] Started that bloody process in my twenties!

Applying for and receiving closed adoption records isn't a straightforward task, well it certainly wasn't back in the nineties. Closed adoptions are a thing of the past, giving way to open adoptions allowing all three parties in the adoption triad (Birth Parents, Adoptive Parents, and the children thereof) more freedom of contact. So where to start? Because I had the forethought to write a diary of the main events during that time, we can go back to 1998. Try not to fall over while the screen goes wobbly!

Twenty-five, married, living in a small terraced house in Nottingham, and I'd been starting to consider more about finding some answers regarding my adoption. To kick things off I went out for a meal one December evening with my parents and broke the news to them. Nervously waiting until we had finished eating before I spilled my beans (I didn't order beans). Of course, they were expecting something like this and were as supportive as I hoped they would be.

My parents informed me that they arranged my adoption through Derbyshire County Council (DCC). Great, I'll start there.

My first goal was getting hold of my adoption records and depending on what they contained, that might be the only goal. Birth parents were told that a closed adoption meant that there would be no further contact with the adopted child by law unless the adoptee wished to trace them personally. Since the 'Adoption and Children's Act 2002', all adoptions in the UK are 'open'. Both adoptive and birth parents must agree to some form of contact that is arranged and agreed upon before the official adoption is finalised.

The internet was very much in its infancy so a lot of the work I needed to do was conducted via letters; face-to-face, at reception desks, on the telephone, or trawling through the Yellow Pages and phone books[6]. 1999 and with a 'New Year - New Me' attitude I phoned Derbyshire County Council (DCC) and was able to get the contact details I needed

I wrote a letter to DCC's County Hall in Matlock, asking for access to my records, popped it in the post box near my house, and settled down to wait. I was expecting months to go by before I heard anything, but on the 13th of January, I received word from them saying that they did have the documents I was requesting. Also included was information about how to apply. DCC asked me to attend a counselling session before my documents could be released and I had to apply to the General Register Office for that. I did this as soon as I could so as not to include any delays of my own doing. And again, settled down to wait.

---

[6] Ok kids, imagine if the internet was in a big book. but with a lot fewer cat pictures in it.

I had to hang on until the 4th of March before a response letter arrived. It contained an application form for counselling and document retrieval, Shit! More delays, I was getting impatient and it had only just started! I needed to chill out a bit.

In May 1999, news that my application had been processed arrived, also stating that I should now wait for a session date to be arranged. So again, I settled down to … pace up and down in my lounge whilst periodically checking the letter box twenty-four hours a day. Six pairs of slippers and four carpets later it was June, and my legs ached! The new letter said that my counselling meeting was set up for the 16th of June 1999. YES! Finally, in less than two weeks I'll have my adoption records! Feelings of relief, excitement, and some apprehension as to the contents of this elusive file, but finally, I was going to be getting my hands on it!

I thought the day was never going to arrive, why did everything seem to come wrapped in so much red tape? I know people had other responsibilities, but never mind all that, this was important, this was my life and I was desperate to know more about it!

I was to meet a social worker at 2 p.m. in the local DCC office near my house, which was a ten-minute walk from home. I can't recall much of the meeting. But the room, I do remember.

It was quite a large space, for an office, and empty, except for two brown moulded plastic chairs placed opposite each other in the centre. There was no desk or table, in fact, no furniture at all. The walls were painted a sea green colour and looking at their condition, that paint may have been applied at the turn of the century.

The space was lit by fluorescent tubes, hanging from the stained '*white*' ceiling tiles, giving off an unusual yellow light, it looked like it had been chain-smoked in for a very long time. The office smelled just as forgotten as it appeared, musty and unclean. It was like sitting in an abandoned hospital. I am aware I should be describing meeting the social worker and our conversation in this potential zombie smallholding, but I don't remember very much beyond how the room looked and felt.

I recall discussing the possibility that any searches for my birth parents or siblings may not be as positive as I hoped and that this meeting was about preparing me for this. I hadn't thought much beyond just getting hold of the documents at this point, but I accepted the advice. I was told that I couldn't take my adoption records away with me that day as they would now have to be prepared, or copied at least. What?! Hadn't they had twenty-six years to do that?

We spent about thirty minutes together dotting the 'i's and crossing the 't's. Me, proving to them that I was of sound mind[7] enough to move forward, while the social worker proved to me that this was not going to be a five-minute turnaround, contrary to my expectations. Bloody hell, these people must have to fill out forms before they can have a lunch break around here!

As she collected her things to end the meeting, she picked up her bag from the floor and pulled out a heavy wedge of A4 paper, held together with a large paperclip. (I still have these documents in the ring binder my file is stored in, and kept the original paperclip too!). I was expecting a roll of red tape to fall out at the same time, with the words "COUNCIL - DO NOT CROSS" printed on it.

She handed me a guide to family tracing as well as a form to complete (surprise, surprise!) to apply for my

[7] I hid it well, before you say it!

original birth certificate. I didn't think of doing that, I wasn't even sure I could. I did have, at that point, a 'Half Certificate'. It's half the size and has my new name typed in good old-fashioned typewriter font across it. To start any search the original birth certificate would be required. As soon as I arrived home, I completed the birth certificate application form and posted it.

After five days, I was back at the abandoned hospital to collect my documents. The same social worker arrived carrying a thick heavy-looking document wallet, and she passed it to me. It felt as weighty as it looked. And I had to resist the urge to squat and spread its contents out across the floor.

Finally, after six months of letter writing; meetings, phone calls, plenty of application forms, some pretty extensive red tape, and waiting, I'd done it!
Now what?

A Big Ball Of Anxiousness

From my perspective, it seems that no matter how our adoptee lives started, or how they continue, most of us appear to end up in the same 'fog'.

I haven't cracked the surface of myself yet. It's as if I'm looking at the problems through a sheet of glass. I know what they are, I can see them, but if I don't take a hammer to that window, I will never get my hands on them. I want to find out what 'Brian the brain's' rewiring has done to me. After all, 'Who's Wally?' is all about me trying to make sense of myself, right?

I used to say that I wasn't an overthinker, I would see it in others and make a point of telling them that it's not something I do, "Nah, I just go with the flow, me." I might say. Ha! Well, I'm going to have to retract that statement. Because it's not true, I've actually spent most of my life overthinking, I've done it so much that it's normal to me. I over analyse, if it's something positive, like for instance I have a practical problem with the car or I have a woodworking project on the go (during lockdown I made guitars), then I'll think the thing inside out. Looking for the best solution, sourcing the materials, and getting it right in my head, it's all I can think about.

Negative overthinking is my special gift though. If I have done something wrong at work, or I've made something I could have done better, or even said something in a conversation that I feel was inappropriate, then I'll fixate on it. I'll carry the thought around with me like a piece of dirty string and play with it until it is an untidy knot in my mind. I'll feel bad about it, ashamed, stupid, and ultimately anxious. Even when I am exonerated, it can take days for me to climb down.

If negative overthinking is my special gift, then overthinking negative scenarios in a relationship is my superpower, and that's the worst part. I can turn a simple thing into a big deal in my mind. Most of the time I know what I'm feeling is incorrect and blown out of proportion, but that doesn't make it less real to me. I'm very good at speaking my mind and being open. However, once I start to overthink, I clam up, I won't speak, keeping it all to myself. If I firmly believed in my thoughts I would share them. But because I know in my heart of hearts it's Brian's fake news, I keep it in, choosing to deal with this cognitive tug-of-war alone. This of course causes the other person to feel they have done something wrong or that I am cross with them.

In some cases, they start to believe I might be seeing somebody else. What other explanation is there for this radio silence from me? Overthinking is not just for the overthinker it would seem. It can be passed on. It messes with more than just the victim of the overthought.

In its heightened form it's called Hypervigilance. And I can relate to this also. I'm always on the lookout for the next problem. The next big pitfall. And it's not always consciously, as in, I don't think I'm aware of how much my mind actually resorts to this type of thinking.

Victims of trauma suffer from hypervigilance, it's a state of permanent high alert. Adoptees have suffered with it all their lives, living with a drop in serotonin and raised adrenaline levels causing the 'fight or flight' response.

The reason I and other adoptees may feel this way could be connected to being relinquished. Our early days of being left alone as a baby for however long was traumatic, it has reprogrammed us to expect to be abandoned by everyone we have close to us. In its extreme form, overthinking leads to anxiety. When my overthinking goes unchecked it spirals out of control, my heart rate increases, my breathing is erratic and I'm off on the anxiety bullet train, speeding through every station on the way to oblivion.

I always describe an anxiety attack as something that comes out of nowhere and takes me by surprise. But perhaps all the signs are there. As soon as I start overthinking, I should be checking my pockets for that train ticket, because perhaps I can get a refund before it's too late.

In conclusion, if I were to give any advice to myself here, I would tell myself that talking is the answer. Don't keep those early stages of overthought to yourself Wally. Swallow your pride and say what's concerning you to someone who will listen. Say it out loud to yourself in the mirror if it helps.

Because the train arriving at platform one will not be easy to disembark.

Incidentally, according to Wikipedia, Serotonin or 5-hydroxytryptamine (5-HT) is a monoamine neurotransmitter. It modulates mood, cognition, reward, learning, memory, and numerous physiological processes. 90% of serotonin, which helps to regulate mood in the body, is generated in the gut where it regulates intestinal movement.

How many of us adoptees suffer from digestive problems?

I know I do. Too much info … ?

"Saturday, Saturday… Sa-turday!"

My best mates during school were Rich and Daz, we had spent most of our early youth either riding or mending our BMX's, often riding around our town with one of us being the custodian of the walkman while the other also had his headphones plugged into it listening to 'Born in the USA' by Bruce Springsteen, God only knows how we pulled that off without serious injury! No, there was often serious injury, still got the scars.

Flann O'Brien in his 1967 book 'The Third Policeman[8]' writes about a policeman loving his bicycle so much he was molecularly connected to it, and I'm sure we had to be surgically separated from our bikes at some point.

---

[8]Written in 1940, but not published, the author withdrew the manuscript from circulation and claimed he had lost it. The book was finally published in 1967. One year after Mr O'Briens death.

It must have been so traumatic that I've blocked out exactly when the procedure took place. Daz moved to our area later but I still have a vague memory of him on a BMX with us.

Even as a child, I liked to keep my life small. I didn't really trust boys, although I had my two best male friends, I think I preferred to make friends with girls. My dad used to say that the girls would all come to me to tell me their problems. I dismissed it at the time, embarrassed, but looking back I think he was right. I'd hear all about boyfriend troubles and fights with parents, I loved it.

Back then of course mobile phone technology was only seen in science fiction, so if you wanted to meet up with people, you either had to phone them on the house telephone or get off your arse and go round to see if they were in.

Sometimes, I'd go around anyway, even if that person didn't answer, just on the off chance they couldn't get to the phone, and it beat doing nothing. Rich's house was at the top of a massive hill. I don't mean standing on its own, as if from a bleak and dark period drama, surrounded by a rickety old fence with crows circling above. I mean, just a hill. However, it wasn't *just* a hill. It was the steepest one on our estate. To my ten-year-old legs, it may as well have been Everest.

The 1984 advert for Raleigh Burner BMX's showed a guy in front of a dramatic sky, all kitted out with the latest full-face helmet and gloves, doing cool freestyle tricks, That's what made you want one. My experience of BMXing was more like attacking steep hills as hard as I could, pulling on the handlebars, and looking to squeeze the last bit of power out of my stick legs. Then coming to a feeble stop halfway up, red-faced, sweating … and walking the bike the rest of the way.

Not quite as cool.

When I did get to Rich's house I was often greeted at the door by his Mum, saying he was already out somewhere. Someone had called for him and he'd gone out with them. What?! How dare he be out with someone who wasn't me! *I* was his best mate, what was he thinking? Then the thought would strike me. "Maybe he's over at my door now," asking my Mum "Is Wally coming out?". I'd race back home, down the now *awesome* hill[9] as fast as I could.

With the bike dumped on the drive outside mine, back wheel still spinning, and the fire brigade sirens ringing in the distance, rushing to attend to the inexplicable strip of flames that was now burning on the streets between the two houses (because I went that fast!), I'd burst through the door shouting "MUM!" "has Rich called for me?"

If the answer was "Yes" I'd fly back out again looking in all the usual haunts to find him.

---

[9] They always are in the opposite direction!

Sometimes I'd find he was part of a big group, hanging around 'The top shops'.

These were a small line of local shops near me, you know the sort, chip shop, newsagents … a knitting shop. That's pretty much all that was there. All you need for a Saturday night in, fish and chips twice, a bottle of wine, a pair of single point number seven knitting needles, and a ball of 20% Aran chunky knit, those were the days.

Once I had seen the group, I often stopped short, watching them from a distance, trying to build up the courage to go over and join in. I was triggered! Not that 'triggered' was the word back then. Why hadn't he called for me? The anxiety of being out of the loop, betrayed by my friend, and the annoyance that I was overthinking, building up inside.

Cut to the back of my head being filmed by the imaginary camera that was recording my life. The gang of kids in the distance over my right shoulder. The camera pulled back, the depth of field distorts as the huge dark sinkhole appears in the street between them and me. I can't get across this void. It's too wide now.

Standing alone holding my BMX up against my side, stuck on one side, them on the other, watching them laughing. I've no choice but to turn away and go home. Angry with myself for losing confidence, angry with him, with them for making me feel like that by just being together and enjoying themselves without me.

I vowed that if they came to call, I would hide so they thought I was out, or I would tell them I wasn't coming out, that would show them. Closing the door after turning friends away like that, just made me feel horrible. Why did I not want to go out? Why was it such a big deal? Go on Wally, get involved. Why did you punish yourself like this? You're not showing anyone anything here, you're just making yourself feel worse and wallowing in your own ten-year-old anxiety and sadness.

That social anxiety is still with me today. It feels exactly the same as it did then. It hurts, I hate it *and* myself for letting it win.

I disliked having to join groups, I just felt out of place, awkward, insignificant and I expected the worst, I still do. I'd find myself doing everything possible to either get away or appease people. Even back then I was a people pleaser, especially if they were the bully type. I'd bend over backward to keep people on my side.

From fourteen to sixteen, my mates and I would spend our Saturday nights drinking in a park local to us, it was our version of a pub. It was the eighties, it's what we all did and we looked forward to it every week. One local newsagent would sell us alcohol, without question. White Lightning cider, Mad Dog 20/20[10], I'd usually get two cans of special brew and a small bottle of dark rum

---

[10] This came out in 1984 and it was a fruit-flavoured fortified wine. All the cool kids drank it.

(yes, I was obviously a dickhead). This would ensure I'd be as drunk as possible for very little funds. I still do that!

We'd take our illegal purchases and congregate on the small adventure playground to get pissed.

There might have been music, I can't really remember, if there was it would have been from someone's Walkman with those little speakers attached. We were often chased into the bushes by the police, no doubt reacting to a noise complaint from the neighbourhood. I can't actually recall us being that loud. Nobody was ever caught, even drunk teenagers were too quick for the 'old Bill'. What is the collective noun for a group of pissed-up teenagers anyway? Just pausing to Ask Jeeves, only joking, I'm Googling it …

Ok, I can't find one for 'Drunk Teenagers' but for Teenagers it's; Clique, Intensity, Mob, Pack, and Tedium.

And for 'Drunks' it's; Load, Stone, and Bender. Therefore, the collective noun for 'drunk teenagers' might be an 'Intense Load'.

I'd almost dread arriving, 'down the park', hoping there would only be a few of us. If so, I was cool, but if there was a larger gathering, I'd be on edge, probably hypervigilant, I just wanted to go home. I never admitted that to my mates at the time for fear of looking weird. If it wasn't for writing this book I don't think I would have realised I did that, but there you go, the power of writing eh?

Once, I was asked by a girl I knew to go to a shop nearby as she didn't want to walk alone. Feeling the wrong side of sober and not really having the inclination, I was going to refuse. I did have to get sober enough to walk the twenty minutes home though (I didn't want to arouse suspicion from my parents), and a walk there might do me good, so I agreed. Having just reached the end of the road, just needing to turn left at the corner, there was a noise behind us.

It might have been someone shouting my nickname "Wally!" I turned to see who it was, there was a loud bang in my head and then it went black.

I woke up laying in the centre of an 'Intense Load' of teenagers with pain in my face and a loud buzzing in my ears. There were kids all standing around me shouting at each other. Where am I? Did I pass out? Why does my head hurt so much? What the fuck had just happened? I remember a wave of anxiety washing over me, my heart was racing. It turned out that I had, as I had suspected, been on the receiving end of a fist to the face, just to the right of my nose and I was knocked out.

It's not clear how long I was out, I'm guessing it was a few seconds, all I remember saying at the time was "But why?" over and over. It transpired that the boyfriend of the girl, had seen me and her walk away from the group and rallied his troops to give me a pasting, just on the off chance we were sneaking off to, as we called it then 'get off with each other'.

The truth was far more innocent than everyone else had considered, and in their teenage drunken states had resorted to the only thing they knew to do, send a big kid to lay me out in the street. Honestly, youth is definitely wasted on the young!

The shouting I had woken up to was high-volume protests of our innocence, and anger towards the meathead who threw his fist without consideration.

The lad apologised to me and it seemed genuine. I should have hit him back, in fact, he suggested I did just that, but I refused. Standing drunk on that street corner, holding my face in case bits started falling off, I forgave him and said it was "No problem". I wasn't even angry, well not on the outside. Even in this situation, with fight or flight on the menu, I chose flight and I backed down, I even started to feel bad for him.

It was around this time that I started to back away from the group and eventually excluded myself completely.

A couple of years later that kid was involved in an accident during his apprenticeship, getting his hand caught in a machine.

I'm somewhat embarrassed to admit that I took some pleasure in that.

Brian has always been working to create a death star-sized anxiety package to be deployed at the slightest threat of large social situations. He's kept my life circles diminutive, only to occasionally allow me to have enough confidence to step out, purely to prove that he was right all along. I'm proud of myself for not retaliating but also, annoyed with my younger self for not standing my ground.

This leads me quite appropriately onto …

Bullying

To me growing up, every kid bigger, or those more confident than me, would make me anxious, and it felt as if I was being physically bullied by these kids constantly. Of course, that's a ridiculous notion, but it's how I felt at the time. Bullying hasn't happened a lot in my life, but it's been there and it's vivid, so it must matter right?

My first memory of being bullied was when I was probably around four years old. Back in 1977, we lived on a Close, in the UK a Close is a street with a dead end, a Cul de Sac. Which, I believe means 'The Arse of the Bag' nice!

I remember playing with other kids on the street, and I remember a mask. A kid a few doors away from my house had a mask, which he/she would wear to scare me, chasing me away. I hated it, I don't remember what it looked like but it was frightening to me.

Was this kid bullying me? The more I consider it, the more I think, yes. It might have been innocent, because it was perhaps hilarious to that person, but that doesn't make it right does it? I guess I need to judge it by my own standards. Would I do that to a four-year-old child? Probably not, but then if I hadn't experienced bullying in my life, if I didn't know how it felt to be the victim, would I then? I suppose I can't answer that truthfully. But I'd like to believe that I was better than that.

The next one that jumps into my head was at primary school. I was in the first year and my antagonist was in the final fourth year.

He made my first year hell. Every playtime he would find me and chase me into a corner, and, for the life of me I can't remember what he did next! I just know I was scared to death by him and I could not wait for him to leave. I hated that first year and playtime wasn't fun for me. It was such a huge relief to little Wally when he finally moved up to the 'big school'.

Oddly, I never saw him again, even when, in 1984 I moved up the ranks to 'big school' myself. Despite the lack of recall, the moments I can remember are always close to the surface, I don't think a week goes by that I don't think about it.

I was fourteen now, it was a Sunday evening, and it was dark out, so it must have been autumn or winter time. I know what you're thinking, "Great details Wally! That's exactly what we need in a book, vagueness!" OK, it was the 11th of October. You see now I don't think you believe me, do you? My sister and I had just been forced to have a bath, and we were sitting in our dressing gowns watching Sunday night TV. Probably Bergerac, with John Nettles speeding around Jersey fighting crime. I'm now humming the theme tune in my head.

There was a knock at the door, not a usual occurrence in our house, especially at that time on a Sunday. My dad went to answer it. A kid I knew was outside on our driveway, he was asking for me.

Dad called me to the door. He and his older mate, who was pacing up and down on the street in front of the house, started yelling at me "You're gonna get smacked" and "I know what you did!" Well, he was way ahead of me, because I hadn't a clue. Apparently, I'd been saying things about his Dad!

That's how it started. It ended with my five-foot, three-inches tall Mum, holding the older kid up against the garage door and shouting directly into his face. My Dad giving the other kid a talking to, while I watched from the doorway, not quite sure what the hell was happening. My anxious stomach was doing flips. I would have ran home if I wasn't already there!

I'd done and said nothing to antagonise these kids, I'd not said anything about his Dad and I didn't even know who his Dad was. The whole thing made no sense to me. All I did know was that I had to go to school the next day … Oh, and my parents were fucking awesome!

Nothing ever came of that night, and nothing was ever said about it at school, but boy was I an anxious ball of a teenager that Monday morning! This event often plays on my mind too, even today. It's obviously had an impact on Brian.

As it turned out, I became an apprentice engineer at the same company that my Mum did her out-work for all those years before. But, my experience was a world away from hers, because I was bullied for years. Every day, by everyone who worked there. Kicked about the place like a used Coke can. I've lost count of the number of times I've been punched, placed in a headlock until I couldn't breathe, or had my hair set on fire (Yes, you read that correctly).

The apprenticeship system in engineering was hard back then, young people were just used as slaves, as well as being ridiculed on a daily basis. Being the youngest employee (I was the last apprentice to be taken on) I was always seen as the 'apprentice' even after qualifying.

I was frightened to ask a question or get anything wrong, fearing repercussions. I'm pleased to say that things are different now, apprentices are treated with much more respect. In 1995, I was asked to go and help out at a different site for the same firm, I couldn't wait to go and that's when it all changed. With around ten members of staff, I was finally treated as a human instead of an unwanted dog, I felt like part of a team instead of part of the problem. Safer. I worked for the company until 1999. I don't think I could have done that if I'd stayed where I was.

In 1997, I'd been instructed to go back to the other site to collect some machine parts in the van. I still hated going over there, but I did as I was asked.

Pulling up I saw a colleague I knew walking up the street. He was probably in his fifties, a heavy-set guy, with ginger hair, glasses, and a beard. If he sounds like a 'Guess Who' Game character to you, then you would be spot on. He was an ex-policeman and hadn't been with the company long.

I opened the window, said "Hello" and joked about him sneaking out of work. He did nothing more than thrust his arm through the open window of the van, grab me by the throat, and squeeze! I'd never had that happen to me before, I thought he was going to choke me to death! Didn't this sort of thing just happen in the movies?

As I sat in the driver's seat of the van, struggling to breathe. He leaned in, told me to "Shut the fuck up!" or something like that, then released his grip and carried on walking.

That massive overreaction to a simple joke frightened the crap out of me. I sat there stunned, what the hell just happened? I've got to follow him inside now! I had another reason to feel anxious about the place. What drives someone to do that to a person? What did he expect to gain from that, my respect? He was going the wrong way about it if that was the case. I'm happy to report that the building has long since been knocked down and is now a row of lovely new three-story townhouses. The factory may be long gone, but the bad memories remain.

Perhaps you are thinking that it was just *that* company and that I was just unlucky? Well, if I was an unfortunate kid then I must have been unfortunate a lot, because during my first year at work, after leaving school, I started my 'Off the job' training. This involved a group of about twelve, sixteen-year-old school leavers working in a workshop learning engineering basics, and it was separated from the normal production workshops in the company.

You'd be forgiven for thinking that I found being in this group difficult. I thought I would too. However, being part of this collection of kids, learning engineering was a great experience. We all got on well, and helped each other get through. We were led through this first year by our tutor. He was an old guy who'd seen a lot of kids come and go under his guidance and he was very good, he pulled no punches, but he was fair and approachable. Also he had the widest thumbs I have ever seen! Put both your thumbs together now … That was one thumb for him! I can still remember being banned from the company canteen on a few occasions because we had invented a game where we would try and stick bits of our lunch to the ceiling, just by throwing stuff skyward. If you're wondering, cucumber slices were the best, but I'm pretty sure someone once managed a slice of white, buttered toast. Still not sure how.

The firm as a whole would have a 'shut down', meaning for two weeks in the middle of summer they closed the entire company, allowing for routine maintenance to be carried out. Because we had a family holiday booked that year, I wasn't eligible for that company-wide break, so I was placed with a department that kept running for the period. This department was run by two members of staff from a small building that made printed circuit boards.

My presence was not welcomed for those entire two weeks. I turned up every morning at 8 am only to be bullied into completing cleaning duties and kicked about continuously until 3.30 pm mercifully arrived. When I look back on that time I can still smell the chemicals that filled the air in the building. If I ever come across similar smells now, I'm taken straight back to those bastards and that awful two weeks. Also, (sorry, there's one more) during that first year of training, we were all placed into local engineering firms to gain three weeks of work experience in real working tool rooms. I was posted to a press shop that made metal parts for car seats.

The tool room/workshop was small and had five employees working as tool makers. This involves machining the tools and platework that fit into the huge presses that stamp out the sheet metal car parts. This is what I was training for. I was really looking forward to it, a chance to have a go at new stuff and see some of what I might be doing day-to-day once

I'd completed my training. My enthusiasm was short-lived.

Instead of being welcomed, guided, and mentored through the working practices of a qualified engineer's daily job, I was ridiculed, bullied, and again pretty much treated like a slave for those three weeks. If I did get any real engineering work to do, it would usually be laughed at, picked apart for faults, and then usually thrown away for scrap. They all seemed to enjoy seeing me fail and had no intention of attempting to help or guide me. I dreaded every day that passed and couldn't wait to be out of there. I did consider complaining, but the aggression and bullying seemed to come from the boss as well as the workshop, so what was the point?

The firm has long since closed down and with any luck those responsible will have died along with it.

What do bullies stand to gain from their actions?

Do they have low self-esteem issues and don't want to be exposed? Do they lower the esteem of others to allow them to rise up the ranks? Sounds plausible. Studies have shown that a bully can have very high self-esteem, and instead use 'Defensive Ego-tism', defending their egos, so as not to appear stupid or small in front of others.

Well, however you slice it, in my opinion, it all comes back to low self-esteem eventually, doesn't it? The person with self-esteem issues picks on the person with self-esteem issues. Just to help with their self-esteem.

I think I've always felt like a victim in my own life. I could be the bully and the victim to myself. Now that is going to take some thinking about.

Am I really bullying myself down? If I am, then why?

I should be the hero in this movie, not the villain or victim.

Lil' Old People Pleaser Me.

"Yes, people pleasing, what's wrong with that, that's a good thing right?" I hear you say. Good people do things for others. I get that. The problem with people pleasing in adoptees is that it comes with a pretty hefty price tag.

For the receiver, it's nothing but good, they have no idea of the real reason behind this good deed.

Long before I came out of the adoption fog I knew, deep down, that I was doing things for others for gratification, to be wanted, recognised, noticed, and even loved. If doing something for someone only came with "Thanks" and not an "Oh my god, that's amazing, you're so good at this, thank you very much!", then I'd be disappointed, hurt, or even slightly angry.

I'd metaphorically arrive in town, all 'Pied-Piper-esque' telling tales of how I can help you in your hour of need, I will remove your rats. I know what I'm doing! All I require in return is your overwhelming gratitude and the knowledge that you will continue to hold me in your heart from now on. Tell me how amazing I am, so that I might feel some self-worth. For I am lacking …

If you don't, I'll kidnap your children.

Ok so, that's where the analogy breaks down, I'm definitely not in the habit of removing children, shit, I'm one of those kids! It was all going so well then there was the awkward kidnapping.

Admitting this to others would usually manufacture a response of "But you're a good person, don't lose sight of that, that's why you do it isn't it?" That's good to know, but no, it's not. Sorry.

Coming from an engineering background and generally being pretty handy I will usually offer to help. I've taken weeks off work to fit kitchens and drove hours to repair someone's car in the rain. I've worked twelve-hour night shifts, then driven to a friend's place to work another eighteen hours for them without sleep.

In some cases, I don't even know how to do the thing that I've volunteered for, I have to learn on the job or research it to death beforehand. That's one of the reasons I steer clear of hospitals. You know, just in case I'm walking past an operating theatre and a nurse bursts out of theatre shouting "Oh no, the surgeon has just collapsed, how will we complete the complicated brain surgery on this poor child now?"

Cut to me scrubbed up, standing head end of a desperately ill eight-year-old child. A scalpel in one hand, rubbing my chin with the other, watching YouTube. There are so many instances of me pushing myself over my limits just for a chance to feel useful, needed, and not a waste of skin.

It's a trait I feel needs to be addressed and is repeated time and time again with adopted individuals. I think for me it is about looking for a place to sit in the world and is linked to not feeling comfortable in myself.

But what is it that drives me and other adoptees to be such relentless people pleasers? Are we all looking to be validated our entire lives? Also, is this just reserved for adoptees or does everyone have a bit of that in them?

Ann Stoneson in her blog 'What makes a people pleaser' writes:

"People pleasing is a strategy for coping with a lack of security in a relationship. While we often focus on the negatives that come with this relational stance, it actually has a lot of strengths in it, too"

This is a great article by the way, and well worth a look.

Oh great! Here it is then, I am a people pleaser because I'm not happy in my own skin. I'm anxious about how I come across to others, I'm insecure in relationships because I feel I'm going to be cast aside again. I have low self-esteem, I want to feel validated and useful and I need to be told so, with gusto please, if you don't mind.

Damn it, I try to write a chapter that goes in a different direction to attachment in relationships, and no matter which way I turn, I'm back where I started!

And all this because one person has an unwanted pregnancy… or three.

Ah, the 1970s eh? What a time to be alive …

I Need To Know - *Part Two*

… Finally after six months of letter writing; meetings, phone calls, plenty of application forms, some pretty extensive red tape, and of course the waiting, I had done it!

Now what?...

Home, and I did just as I had the urge to do in the council office and spread the paperwork out on the floor of the dining room. Then the table and the odd chair here and there. There was so much. Visit reports, case studies, medical reports, and notes about meetings, were all mixed up together and nothing chronological at all. Some of the documents had been skewed in the photocopier and might have had important information accidentally cropped off, I couldn't tell. Plus, why did they find it so difficult to add the date to formal documents back then?

I started to try and arrange the papers correctly, searching for clues as to when the file or report was created in the sometimes barely legible handwriting, but I soon got bored. So I slid it all into clear plastic wallets and secured them in a green A4 ring binder. And that is how it has stayed. The first thing I wanted was clarity on who my birth parents were. I still had no idea whether I wanted to find them, but that didn't deter me from needing to know.

After spending more time that evening perusing the folder, I started to realise that the reports included social worker's personal opinions. Not just of the facts but opinions of the people involved. Sometimes the notes contained observations of whether or not that person was good-looking, indifferent, likeable, or not likeable for that matter. This surely wouldn't be entertained today.

By the end of the day, I had a lot of key information to go on, such as; birth mum and dad's full name and birth dates, last known addresses, and my birth mum's latest boyfriend. Who, she was engaged to. That means she may have been married to him. Sure enough, with a bit more sleuthing, I found a report dated January 1974 that said she had indeed been married. Right, now, I have an eight-month window between May 1973 when I was born, and January 1974, when the report was created. there has to be a record of their wedding for this period.

As I knew that her last recorded address was in Sheffield, I fired up the clockwork internet before going to bed and found the address of the Sheffield Archives, which was, and still is located on the first floor of Sheffield's Central Library on Shoreham Street. If there is any information on this wedding, then I'll find it there.

The next day I awoke to a very wet and rainy Tuesday. I'd booked some time off work after picking up my records because I had intended to get 'Miss Marple' and be all over this searching malarkey. When I say Miss Marple, I mean in a younger, more masculine way. Perhaps Sherlock Holmes may have been a better reference here. Well, they both wore a hat.

Sheffield Archives was 41.7 miles from my house and just less than an hour away up the M1. I just checked the mileage, it's not a fact I remember, I'm not quite that Sherlock. It was raining there too. After explaining my intentions to the staff, I was ushered over to the microfiche machines, surrounded by old heavily varnished drawers all containing records dating back to god knows when, the Big Bang I assumed. It was explained where to look for the records I needed and I was left alone. I finally found the slide I needed and slid the film into the machine.

I scanned through and found the records that could contain details of the marriage I was looking for … Damn it. It's double-printed!

I went back and checked the previous page, It was fine, but there was no mention of it. I went forward beyond the double-printed page, and again, nothing to report. So it's got to be right in between the two good pages. I tried looking again, but it was no good, it was just a nebulous fuzz on the screen in front of me. But hang on, what about the spares? These can't be the only copies on-site.

I asked at the desk. "I'm sorry, we only have one copy of each of these records". I deflated a little. Ok, "Do you expect to get another copy anytime soon?" I asked. "We get new copies supplied to us every five years," they said. More deflation. Perhaps though, these records were four years and eleven months old. A new set could be arriving any day now, yes? No, the records were only three months old. Oh balls!

The last bit of air in my metaphorical balloon squeaked out.

Never mind, 'Rome wasn't built in a day', 'there are more ways to skin a cat' and as important as this was to me, 'I was just a small cog in a large wheel' here. Incidentally, I've just written an entire sentence using only idioms and you didn't even notice, or did you just 'turn a blind eye'? I'm sorry, 'I don't want to upset the applecart' Oh bloody hell, now I can't stop it!

Of course, I did as you would have expected, I got straight back on the horse, right? (Is that another one? Now that was unintentional). Wrong. My first stumbling block and I just tripped over it and gave up, vowing to return to it as soon as I could. What an anticlimax. However, it's not all bad news, I did receive my original Birth Certificate a month later.

Even though I'd stopped searching, I occasionally looked at the folder and I happened upon the address of my first foster parents in the file. I was transferred to them at around ten days old. I'm being more vague here, due to my lack of note-taking at the time. I pulled out the BT phonebook. Back then, they were huge and I remember seeing strong men on the TV ripping them in half to prove some kind of point. It would be really easy now, the last one I received was three years ago and it was more like a leaflet that said "We don't know, just bloody Google it, will you?"

Amazingly, they were still listed in the book. I called them that day. They were still married and had two children of their own. They were very surprised to hear from 'David'. I explained that I was Andy now and that I had a happy childhood overall. They told me that I was the first and only child they ended up fostering, because during the few weeks 'David' was with them, they found out they were pregnant, so chose to discontinue fostering.

It wasn't a long call, just a few minutes. I thanked them for being there for me in the first few weeks, they wished me luck in my search before saying goodbye. This was a lovely moment and I was left almost overflowing with emotions, excitement, happiness, and sadness, almost in sympathy for baby me. It was at this point that I parked my search and hung up the deer-stalker hat. It stayed on the peg for almost four years.

In those four years, I made a few changes. A new wife, a one-year-old son, and a new job. The new wife had come with the job as she was a fellow employee of the same firm. After a joke text sent to her by a colleague from my phone, suggesting I fancied her (unbeknown to me I might add), we ended up on a date and that was that. Well that showed him, because we were together for nearly nine years and had two kids together. I have often thanked him for that interjection. As the years went on the green folder burned brighter and brighter in my mind until I had no other choice than to start looking again.

I don't know what turned the switch, perhaps it was the fact that I was now a father myself but I had an ever-increasing desire to find my birth mother. The internet was growing and Friends Reunited was the big thing. It was an early Facebook of sorts I guess. In November 2003 I set up an account and started to search for names of my birth family. Nothing, no results. Perhaps all this new social media had got some catching up to do eh? It'll never take off you know!

It didn't take me long to start looking for online tracing websites. One that I engaged with was called Searchline. I've just done a quick Google search for it but all that comes up now are links to petrochemical companies and gas detection devices. It's clearly been taken down now. On the message board, I placed a post. "My name is Andrew Wallis, my birth name was 'Dave Charles Rice' and I am looking to find my birth mother. Her name is … she was born … blah blah" you get the idea. Initially, I was requesting an idea of the cost for them to do this work for me, so I was expecting a call or an email regarding that sort of thing. The first form of correspondence I received was definitely not what I was expecting.

A lady rang my mobile phone while I was at work. She introduced herself and I confirmed that it was indeed I that had posted on the message board and that I was looking for an idea of cost. "Well, " she said, "Your birth Mum". Mistaking this for a question, I said, "Yes please,my birth Mother …"
As I tried to continue, she cut me off mid-sentence.

"We've found her".

Corrupted Code

I'm not a medical professional, I'm not a professional anything for that matter, although I was a professional photographer for about ten years. Having the ability to take a good photograph, or 'Make' a photograph as we 'togs' like to say, is not very conducive to writing about the intricacies of the adoptee's mind in a scientific way, so I won't. What I will do, however, is learn about myself and my link to adoption and the potential trauma within, and try to recognise what my issues are.

Adoption trauma manifests itself in lots of ways it would seem. From the obvious emotional stuff like anxiety and depression, to the less obvious social quirks like refusing to do something fun because it wasn't the adoptee's idea. Weird as it might seem, I can recall lots of moments in my past where I've just flatly refused an activity or outing for fear of losing the element of sovereignty.

This often leads to a 'Brian' driven anxiety attack. I'd get so worked up before the event that I'd lose it and then panic about the loss of control, which in turn would create its own loss of control. Finally topped off with a nice big dollop of shame to boot. 'Dollop' great word that!

I could never explain why I felt the way I did, or where it all came from. It was highly confusing to me and others involved. There are physical symptoms too, and not just from the anxiety. Yes, the digestive issues. As I've become older, did I mention I am fifty now?

Yes, as I've become older I'm less tolerant of certain foods. One, in particular, is oats. I won't go into too much detail here, but needless to say,

I don't get a great deal of enjoyment during the post-oat consumption hours.

Now, this could well be a part of getting on a bit or the fact that there was a period of time a few years ago when I pretty much lived on flapjacks! That said, there is no getting away from the fact that some adoptees who feel they are living with adoption trauma, also report similar physical symptoms.

Above all else though I fear the most obvious issue I have is with attachment. My past is littered with broken friendships and relationships that, almost without exception, were down to me. With any new relationship, I tend to go all in, right from the off. Telling myself that I'm sick of restarting, so this time it will be different. I will be better. I'm being the person I want to be and getting that across to the recipient, leaving no room for error. My head is light and airy and the world is full of possibilities. I feel weightless and life is fun.

But, there is a possibility that due to being relinquished by my birth mother in that first week of my life, my mind could be predisposed to think that everyone close to me is temporary, that I'm going to be left alone again at any moment.

Our minds are thinking machines, and those machines spend all day relaying information like; "Oh, look at the size of that dog, what's for dinner tonight" and "God, I hope that smell isn't me!" and when we have conscious thoughts in this way, we know our minds are working, helping us.

There is also the sort of workings that we don't necessarily see flashing across our heads. And they are the ones that allow us to be breathing and driving the car at the same time. Or, doing as I am now, thinking of phrases for this paragraph and being able to type it out, delete it, and type it out differently. Then fix all the typos.

Read it out loud and say "Nah", without physically needing to direct my hand to the correct letter on the keyboard. Amazing stuff, humans are very well adapted. Yes … But …

There's the other stuff our brains do and that also happens without conscious thought. The chemical stuff.

This clever stuff gets involved to help us feel happy, balanced, and level. Frightened, sad, or worried. It makes sure that we react in the right way based on a predetermined set of rules or 'software' that our brains have stored. As soon as we physically experience something, our brains trigger the correct chemical mix to help us through. There is a school of thought suggesting that it happens the other way around. Our brains are pre-empting the situation and start their signalling before the event. It all happens so fast that we just don't notice.

This is all great news of course, as long as your software isn't corrupted. Psychotherapist, Tony Ingham, in his blog 'Adoption Trauma in Adopted Adults', describes an adoptee's cognition in this way:

"As children, as part of ordinary development, we might build up a sense of the world around us that we then go on to internalise. We can then carry that picture in our minds, and it provides us with the psychological coordinates we need to live, work, and thrive. It nurtures us. Certain events, such as adoption, can damage this internal model and the problems that result from that are enduring and go on to be the origin of complex problems in our lives."

Clever eh? I liked this description so much, I contacted Tony and asked if I could quote him in my material. He agreed, I didn't steal it, honestly… he also asked if I could share a link to his work. You can find details of where to find this particular article at the back of this book along with other useful stuff.

Internalising our birth trauma through relinquishment has allowed Brian to lay some pretty dodgy-looking foundations for me to build my walls off (often that's exactly what they are, walls). Causing me, and many other adoptees, no end of troubles throughout life. I'm hoping it ought to be easy enough to demolish, just need the right-sized hammer.

On Christmas Day, 2021, I bought football goals and a new ball for my partner's son. In the afternoon it was decided that we would use them at the local park.

Goals were set up and the game started. There was no room for me as it was two versus two. So I was told to be the referee. "Fair enough," you say, right? Not to Brian it wasn't. I started feeling very much on the outside, looking in. Eventually, my mood fell and I walked off. Just to be on my own. I was gone for over an hour.

When I eventually returned, I was very quiet and just sat reading, all the time trying to work out what had happened and why. Where had that come from?

It arrived all of a sudden and brought my mood right down extremely quickly. Did the software in my head start running the 'You're being abandoned again' routine? Surely not. I mean how? Why? It was just a simple family game of football. I should have been enjoying the fact that my gift was getting used and bringing happiness, shouldn't I? The answer of course, is yes. At the time I had no clue as to what was going on.

I felt very insignificant and almost embarrassed because of how I reacted. It's only through interacting with other adoptees, the research and writing that I am doing, that I can now look back on that moment with a bit more clarity. I firmly believe that my inability to process attachment is the reason for this little drop in power. And that blows my tiny little broken mind!

Trauma. That's the corruptor. Many people suffer trauma from something terrible that has happened to them at some point in their lives, but they may have had many years of pre-trauma. They can look back and pinpoint where the changes took place. But with myself and no doubt other adoptees, the trauma of abandonment by the birth mother happened so early on in their lives that, as Nancy Verrier puts it in her book 'Coming Home to Self' there is "no pre-trauma self" to call on. The theory being that my reactions to some scenarios could be skewed because Brian is using different rules.

So, how can we possibly trust ourselves to act 'normally'? The short answer is we can't. Strange emotional responses should be expected. The super-power here though is understanding these responses and heading them off at the pass.

Shutting down the software before it starts making these changes, understanding that they happen, and being able to sense the trigger is very powerful.

If Love Ain't Enough

Sunday. Just the thought of it, when you say it, *screams* relax. Ok, it doesn't literally scream relax, it is Sunday after all. But while some in the UK are recovering from last night's excess, mowing the lawn, washing the car, or out for Sunday lunch, I am sleeping, trying to catch up from the lack of sleep offered to me by the previous night shift.

Then while those same people are settling down to a nap in front of the TV, I'm driving to work. And then, while people are... Ok, ok, you get the idea, *I'm working!*

Yes, I'm one of the lucky few that gets to work on a Sunday night. But wait … the best bit is, I also get to work right through until 6 am Monday. Can you imagine that? A whole twelve-hour night shift. On a Sunday, what a treat!

I know what you're thinking. What a fortuitous life he leads. I wish I was him! However, I will be driving home to bed while most people are doing the Monday morning commute and that is a nice feeling.

I usually, not always, but usually listen to a book or a podcast on the way to work. Music, as endless and varied as it is, gets a bit boring. I know that sounds weird and I might be a little odd, don't ask me how. It just does.

If I get bored of listening to music that someone has already conveniently made for me, then I'll just make my own music on guitar. I don't record much of it and if I do it's usually via the voice recorder on my phone. I've been playing guitar now for around twenty years and I'm ok at it. I wouldn't say I was great, just ok, and that's fine with me. I have no desire to be better.

I get what I want out of it and playing to an audience of dust mites and house spiders is my kind of crowd. Unfortunately, some of them leave early, due to hearing the same song over and over for twenty minutes straight while I sit working out all the chords and strumming patterns. Hey, it's their loss.

I do love being able to play an instrument, it's one of the few times that my mind slows down. An hour sitting with a guitar is not an hour wasted, although that hour will go by in the blink of an eye. I've often sat and played for a whole afternoon feeling that time had stood still only to realise it had done quite the opposite. I feel similar about writing. Time flies by and I just lose myself. It's not easy being an anxious ball of hypervigilance most of the time, so a bit of respite in something creative is a great relief.

Most of my guitar-playing repertoire lives in the Indie/Britpop camp. I like it, and I'm a lazy player. The chords are usually pretty standard and are easy to pick up. Unlike Jazz chords where you need two extra fingers, Oasis tunes, and Noel Gallagher's music, in particular, is a go-to for me and I can normally get my fingers around one of their tracks within a few minutes. I was in my twenties when Oasis arrived on the scene and so either of the Gallagher brothers' material has a place in my heart.

So there I was, driving the thirty miles to work. Minding my own business, as you do in the car, and for a change I was listening to music, a bit of Noel Gallagher's, High-Flying Birds. The third track of Noel's album, Council Skies started playing called, If Love Ain't Enough.

My mind, on permanent hypervigilance by default, put its foot to the floor and lit up my synapses like a Christmas tree. Flashing years of my life across my eyes, the most recent stuff first. I saw Em and me. Where we were, and where we are now. The moments of Brian the brain madness in between, the chapter Looking From The Outside In, Em has written and her letter 'Dear Wally'.

Other relationships now, everything speeding up, How they ended, and how it all looked like it was all down to me. Faces, moments, sadness, happiness. It was all coming at me like race cars on a track. The words, phrases, and paragraphs from the book and the blog came charging forward, good things, and a sense of pride for the writing. Then bitterness that I've got this inside me at all.

Then all the weird and not-so-good things that have made up a ragtag collection of disasters and successes followed. I don't like this, I don't like it at all!

The music took me to the guitars I have hanging on my living room wall, and how I've neglected them of late due to being so engrossed in writing. I felt good and ashamed of myself all at the same time. The song continued to play out …

I thought "That's me. It's all me." Isn't it odd how songs have a habit of triggering you?

Why is love not enough? Do I subconsciously request being left dead to the world because of my stupid self-esteem issues? Am I asking myself whether love is enough? I know it *should* be.

Images, memories, questions, over and over again, as if I was seeing a movie play in fast-forward, but still able to get an idea of the plot. Just when I thought it was never going to end, my face felt hot and I felt tears well up in my eyes. While I was being bombarded by thought, the song continued on.

Now I was struggling to see the road. I wiped my eyes with the back of my hand and drove on.

Wow. That was weird, I felt odd, shaky, anxious, hot, and bewildered.

Five minutes later and I was doing it again. I felt my shoulders start moving and I knew I was in danger of sobbing to the point at which road safety would become an issue. I regained my composure, briefly. This time it was almost a full-on lament. I'm in danger of properly losing it and I needed to get myself together, I have to work a twelve-hour shift! Thankfully it did subside and I was able to turn in for work without mascara running down my cheeks, fanning my face with my hand, whilst simultaneously blowing invisible tubes of air through pursed lips. I'm joking, I don't wear mascara, not on a workday.

I've been looking inside myself a lot, I've pulled some very emotional stuff out of my head, and I've done so almost as if I was writing about somebody else. I'm pouring all this out, and up to this point, I haven't cried a single tear.

It's great to be finally getting the words out, but it did seem a little strange that I had failed to connect properly to the emotions. I just figured it was because I was making sense of it and was starting to find some peace, and that may be so to a point.

Yes, I'm finally standing on the imaginary, emotional see-saw, but being able to stand at the centre of it and achieve equilibrium is the goal, and I'm obviously not there yet. Plus I am completely in the dark as to how many steps it will take to get there.

So why am I having this mini-breakdown? My estimation is thus. I'm working on the editing every day. I'm reading the book, seeing the facts, thoughts, feelings, and emotions I've written about me and what goes on inside Brian for the first time ever, and it's pressing my buttons. Music could be channelling this and subconsciously helping me to access the emotional responses I've kept locked away for too long.

It's all there in front of me now, everything I've avoided facing, and it's only through reading my own words back, often out loud (to aid writing flow and clarity), that it's having an impact on me. I'm starting to see things for what they truly are. I've opened that 'primal wound' everybody talks about, it's bleeding and it's likely to get messy.

'Dear Brian,

Thanks for the info and all that, but could I request that you perhaps choose a time that's more suitable to start these processes? Rather than when I'm hurtling into a tight bend on a country road at sixty miles per hour. Thanks awfully!'

The Other Viewpoint

I've talked about how adoption trauma has influenced my life. But what if it hasn't?

So many adoptees suffer the effects of being given up by their birth mothers, believe it's connected and do our best to work through and understand it. However, I'm asking, what if it is something else?

After the research and learning that I have done recently, I'm a convert. I believe that a lot of my issues have been influenced by my relinquishment many years ago.

For the chance to explore, and for balance to my beliefs, I thought it would be a good idea to look at the theories around at the opposite end of adoption trauma.

There isn't very much out there to the contrary. 99% of adoption trauma-related information (not a true calculation in case you were wondering, just flying by the seat of my pants) out there in Internet-land say it's a thing, but let's look at the 1%. There is no smoke without fire, right? Except for maybe fireworks and when you try to burn evergreens. I mean, that's ALL smoke!

Starting with the phrase "Adoption trauma is not real" I searched Google. Ten pages in and nothing! Not even a slight mention of any opposing view. Ok, not to be put off, I tried "There is no such thing as adoption trauma". Again ten pages into Google and still nothing! Oh, I expected many more hits than I was seeing, so I tried again and this time typed "I don't have adoption trauma", on the first page and three organic results down, I found something on Adoption.com. Finally.

The article has been written by an adoptee and a mother. As an adoptee, she wasn't "snatched away and left with strangers" but "laid in loving arms". As a mother, it appears she suffered an extremely difficult pregnancy. There is nothing in the article that suggests reasons why this person believes there was no trauma for her. The article does go on to talk a little more about DNA-based trauma though. This is a type of trauma believed to be hereditary and handed down through generations. Experiences during pregnancy could have been transferred to her son deep in his DNA. It suggests that, if the mother is suffering then the unborn child would suffer too and be born with trauma. Again this was not the case for her either.

There are a few discrepancies between my adoption records and my birth mother's recollection concerning exactly how long I was actually with her in hospital after my birth.

It could have been a few days or I might have been taken from her directly.

I don't think I'll ever know now. I do know however, that I was placed in the care system after around ten days for a few weeks before I was finally transferred to be initially fostered by my new parents awaiting the formal adoption process. I guess what I'm getting at here is that I don't believe I was truly "snatched away" either, yet I feel I've been living with a form of relinquishment trauma all my life. Furthermore, I feel that I'm not in the minority either.

The DNA trauma mentioned is a fascinating subject. The article asked how can a person suffer trauma if they didn't experience it? And here is where I think the article's theories get a little skewed. In all the research I have, and am continuing to do, it seems to me that adoption trauma does not start before birth. But rather in the first few weeks afterward. As infants, humans are born with a very underdeveloped brain.

Our brains then spend around three years growing and have to start working before they are completed.

The first month of an infant's brain is a critical time and it is in this period that we lose the only thing our narcissistic little minds need, Mum. Yes, it's all me, me, me for us here. Of course, it is during this time that the trust gets destroyed.

I'm not saying that I don't believe DNA trauma isn't a thing, I'm saying I'm not entirely convinced it's related to adoption. But I'm happy to be proved incorrect here. Incidentally, I watched a brilliant TedX Talk a few months ago about this very subject. Leah Warshawski tells a beautiful story about her Grandmother and her experiences as a Jewish child during World War II. She believes that her experiences during this time have been handed down to her. It's really worth a watch.

In conclusion, there has been so much work done, by so many confirming the existence of adoption trauma, but very little suggesting otherwise. I feel much more confident moving forward with my quest.

Andy The Android

A lack of self-esteem can do strange things to me. Am I good enough? Did I say the right thing? Oh god! Did I say the wrong thing? So when I love someone, I fall fast. I do everything in my power to make sure that person knows how I feel at every opportunity. I think I need to know that the other person in the relationship knows I'm serious. Perhaps to me, if I lay my heart out then there's less chance of them leaving me.

But then later down the line, I lose momentum, I start to question myself and my position in this other person's life. Why me? I'm just not good enough. Why are they wasting their time? They deserve better. Then everything becomes a mountain to climb and I start to shut down.

Eventually, I close off completely, shutting off communication. Text messages become short and few, and I do as much as I can to put the other person out of my head because it hurts to think about them. If I do think about them, and to be perfectly honest, it's just as often as I did when I was feeling good about 'us' so who am I kidding here? It comes with a pressure that I physically feel in my head. I have visions of them talking about me with friends and laughing about how ridiculous I am. Then Brian does his best to raise the issues of low self-esteem.

After all that has happened, and this can take weeks by the way, I turn into Andy the android. I lose all feeling. I feel no emotion at all, as if I've locked it away in a box in my head, then swallowed the key.

Emotional numbness as it is often referred to, is a symptom of stress or anxiety, depression, fatigue, post-traumatic stress disorder, or medication.

So how could I possibly explain it when it happens to me?

I guess the first thing to do is to explain how it feels. It is as if I have a sheet of glass between myself and the world. I'm a squash court wall, and everything else that could and should create an emotional response from me is the ball, and it bounces off. Actually, that's not quite the case, only things that are directly related to myself seem to get filtered out. For example, a meaningful conversation with a loved one that might require an emotional response. Nothing, flat, nada, I'm a blank sheet of paper. But sit me in front of a movie and I cry like a baby! It almost makes no sense.

But hold on a minute, perhaps there is something in this. You see, it's safe to cry at a movie as there's nothing remotely related to me in it, I don't have to let go of the emotions that I'm protecting in that box.

None of this is me, so I can just let go of it. It's worth noting also that because it's not opening the tap that are my true emotions, then there is no real relief from that release. Good, I've kept control. Well of course that's not good, but during those times, it feels good. Yes, I know that sounds odd. That's how it works. For me at least.

But, why am I numb?

For me, it starts with a growing feeling of threat. My relationship with this person is threatened. Not in a physical sense, just an underlying feeling. Where that threat comes from is from others outside of the 'us'. All those friends and social arrangements the other person has and does. That's a horrible feeling to have because I know that a healthy social life is key to feeling happy and I want that for the other person, of course. But isn't that just taking them away from me? Soon they will realise that I am an idiot and I'm holding them back. A large social scene is something I don't really allow for myself.

127

I feel safer in smaller circles, so there must be a dose of jealousy in there too as I really wish I felt capable of such things.

Oh look, here comes Brian again with his suitcase full of low self-esteem.

I do spend a lot of my time generally on high alert, on the brink of the fight or flight response. General Anxiety Disorder I was told when I signed up for some online Cognitive Behavioral Therapy (CBT) last year, during another particularly low spot. CBT is great at combating the symptoms, but does not address the roots of the issues. I'm not suggesting it shouldn't be tried however, go for it. It helps. But it's a bit like topping a car engine up with oil without fixing the leak.

The ability to regulate emotions is something that Nancy Verrier refers to in her book 'Coming Home to Self' as something that is directly related to mood. The book also discusses the fact that this regulation is often linked to the presence of overwhelming feelings and I can definitely relate to that.

Those overwhelming feelings will ultimately trigger the suppression of emotion. Being a negative and anxious thinker by default, I'm always on the lookout for the next disaster, or hypervigilance as it's better known. Hypervigilance is common in adoptees, being born into a world we cannot trust because the only person in that world that we needed is gone, Mum. I do find the whole concept tricky to swallow at times because I don't remember any of it.

However the evidence is out there, you only have to type 'Adoption Trauma' into Google to see it, pages and pages of articles, books, podcasts, and Facebook groups, You name it.

I'm a robot, controlled by a program created long before I was aware it was being installed. Version

One of that code is out of date, Version Two is
coming and it's going to change the operating system.

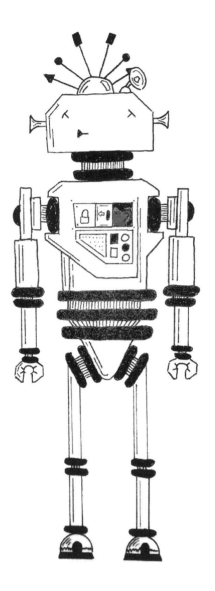

A Style Flexing Chameleon

'Style flexing', I first heard the term a few years ago while I was working at a previous job. The firm had a huge spread across the globe, acquiring company after company, with thousands of employees, or 'stakeholders' as they preferred to call them. They were, and still are, to my belief, an American family-owned business, and 'family' seemed to be a big word for them. They wanted to create a culture within the business that embodied the notion of family. "Everybody matters" was the phrase that paid around there. Literally.

I was sceptical, and I wasn't alone. Quite a few of my British colleagues struggled to take the whole thing seriously. American business cultures just seem to rub us Brits up the wrong way at times.

In my opinion, they have a habit of rebranding common sense, and then turning it into an arse-numbing three-day PowerPoint. The British like to turn up, clock on, do the work and then clock off. Let me get on with what you pay me to do, don't involve me with too much of the cuddly stuff and you won't get many complaints.

Oh look, I'm attending a three-day course! Before the course, we all had a personality quiz to complete, a bit of light sanding to expose the grain in the wood that was our personality. From that we were assigned a letter A, B, C, or D. These corresponded with a personality type. Essentially highlighting the go-getters and the procrastinators, or the fiery and placid. My letter was…. Well, I don't know, because I didn't do that bit. Probably a mini-protest. I feel they might have had to add a new letter for me anyway.

This, however, was the way they taught us all about style flexing, telling us how to communicate effectively with an 'A' if you were a 'D' and so on.

Over the course of the entire first day they chose to inflict this one subject upon us. I came to realise, in between naps, that this was just common sense, don't we all do this flexing? Mostly without realising what we are doing. It is actually how we communicate with others, it's often a subconscious shift in our personalities that allows us to converse, work, or get along with the majority of people in our lives. How many of us leave out the swear words when talking to our parents, teachers, or work colleagues? I would suggest it's most of us, that's style flexing at work. Bringing yourself up, or sometimes down, to try and interact equally with someone.

It happens even more if you're going to that person for a favour, advice, or with a difficult question.

It helps you to get the result you're looking for. Sneaky eh? Adoptees have a problem however, they were given up at birth, and this 'little event' helps to nurture mistrust and leaves us with an underlying fear of being rejected, again. It can make us flex our styles to the extreme. It's often referred to as being like a Chameleon. Chameleons change the colour of their skin to suit their environment and blend in, it's not just a defense mechanism, it's like their mood ring too.

My experiences as an adoptee definitely reflect this. I am insecure socially. I feel out of place, insignificant and not required, or tolerated. So I try really hard to say the right thing or act the right way. I am constantly monitoring how the interaction is going, as if I'm trying to keep a saucepan of soup simmering and not boiling, just stirring and watching, turning up or backing off the gas, hoping not to burn the best bits to the bottom of the pan.

If I feel a disconnection, I lose confidence, and I begin to feel that others are irritated by my inclusion. I eventually retreat and become quiet, hoping I don't annoy anybody from then on. It often takes me a lot to overcome this and dive back in. It's exhausting.

I've spent so long flexing that I'm not sure who I am anymore. If I ever knew.

In my working life, I've been in some form of engineering role since I was sixteen years old. That's thirty-four years and counting. But I feel it's almost reluctantly. I have a very busy and creative mind and it's led me to do lots of other things over the years. Trying to find 'me'? Perhaps. Looking for who I really am? Possibly.

I've never considered myself a proper engineer. It's just what I've been able to get away with while being paid. However, since turning thirty I've been a painter and decorator, a wooden floor fitter, a professional photographer, a web designer, a teacher, a guitar maker, and now I'm a writer. All these jobs were side hustles and don't they just scream *"This guy has no idea who he is?"*

When I recently told someone I was a maintenance engineer, they were surprised. Expecting me to be doing something that was more akin to the arts due to my creative spirit. As you know, my birth name was David and I've always maintained that David died when I was adopted and Andy lives on. Perhaps though, Andy is the engineer and David is the arty creative one, or visa-versa. He's not dead at all. He's still here, living a parallel life but in the same dimension.

Style flexing in relationships is something that must be very common. Laughing at your new partner's jokes, even though you may have had funnier headaches. Or, agreeing to see a show they love because you want to appear supportive and interested in their life, but all the time wondering if it might be possible to go in disguise, just in case your mates catch sight of you. We do it out of love for that person, but isn't there a part of us that feels it makes the journey together a little easier too?

In relationships, I take it to the next level and try to be what I believe the other person expects, not that I'm aware that I'm doing it at the time. Of course, the truth is, the other is more than happy with who I am to begin with.

In the past I've gone from being an avid TV watcher to someone that hates having the TV on. I've thrown away furniture that I'd previously spent hours restoring, so as to change it to a new style, just because it wasn't to the other's taste. I've even become a smoker again after years of abstinence just because the new partner smoked. I lose my identity in a heartbeat for the chance to be with someone.

I've heard from a lot of partners, "You are an enigma." Of course I'm an enigma to them: the person they first met is changing in front of their very eyes, altering his skin colour to suit the new environment.

And for what?

Adoptees already know what I'm going to say next I'm sure, All together now!

"Because I don't want to be left alone again!". Why do I always end up on my own then … Eh?

Incidentally, Chameleons also have really long powerful tongues and extremely sticky spit ...

So don't go asking me to lick an envelope. Oh, and a prehensile tail … Leave it.

5k a day? You Idiot!

For approximately ten years the side hustle was Professional Photographer, it was a business born out of a hobby. I was asked to photograph a wedding for a work colleague, that one shoot became two, then three, then hundreds! In the last couple of years, the business had grown and I was a busy fool, doing lots of work, for little gain. Simultaneously, I had weddings, corporate, studio, and product photography. There was also a photography training school that I had developed, as well as a camera club.

On top of that, I had built a photo booth for events that I was driving around the country. Which sounds a lot for one person to manage right? If you couple that with also working a full-time engineering role, and all the photo business admin, then it gets even more crazy. I look back now and wonder how the hell did it. Eventually, I begrudged the time it consumed and I closed the business in 2015.

One part of the photography business was event photography. I've photographed brides and grooms, supermarket openings, dog food, skydivers, celebrities and royalty. I'm not really much of a Royal family fan, and putting them after dog food just there, should have given it away. My favourite part, and the most rewarding (adoptees need to have those rewards), was donating my time as a photographer to a local hospice, shooting fundraisers. They really appreciated my efforts and I loved to do it. I guess it satisfied my need to please and be accepted.

Then one day it wasn't enough and people pleasing went to a whole new level.

I wasn't much of a sports fan growing up, at seven-years-old I was forced to play football for my Cub Scout pack.

It was early 1981 and a freezing cold, grey, and drizzly day with my Mum and Dad on the touchline spurring me on. I was in right-wing defense and this suited me completely as our opponents were poor and our players spent much of the first half as far away from our goal as it was possible to get.

I loafed at the back watching the ball intensely from a distance, making sure I had time to swerve out the way of any oncoming play. I felt extremely out of place, completely useless, and totally on the outside looking in. It was miserable, and I hated it. Not surprisingly, I didn't play the second half. Good!

So, to find myself becoming a runner towards the end of 2010 was quite odd. I hated that too. Truly hated it, I still do. But I was feeling overweight for my height at that time, or maybe I was just too short for my weight. Whichever way you chose to see it, I felt unfit, fat, and old!

I trained for, and completed a half marathon, which I dramatically underestimated, nearly giving up at the seven-mile mark and coming in with an awful time of two hours and forty-five minutes. However bad that experience was, I kept going with the running, getting out a few times a week. Ok, maybe once a week. Did I mention I hate running?

In 2013, I had a bit more enthusiasm for running and was making good steady progress, I'd lost some of the weight and had lots more energy. I decided that I was going to try another half marathon and cross the finish line in under two hours. So I was serious. But how could I keep the momentum going with my training? An idea formed.

Back to my next level people pleasing moment. One night, I sent an email to the hospice I was volunteering for as an event photographer.

"Date: Monday 21st October 2013 – 11.53 pm

To: Kate – Notts Hospice

Subject: 5k a day (At Least)

Hi Kate,

I saw that someone was doing a running challenge for a local charity and it gave me an idea…

It's basically this:

I will run 5K (at least) every day for a year. I'll even run the Nottingham Half Marathon as part of it. I would also run some park runs; they are usually 5K.

I was also thinking that people/businesses whatever, could suggest weird places to cover 5k (it has to be using my legs though). It would be a great way to raise awareness and funds for you, but I will wait to hear your thoughts first.

Thanks,

Kind Regards, Andy"

As I get older I realise that I have an impulsive side but that was the summit of Mount Impulse, I spent no time at base camp perusing the foothills, plotting my route at all. "Hi, I'm here to scale Mount Impulse... see you in a bit. The top is this way right?"

My spontaneity stands pretty much alone in our family and usually comes up against worried eyes and some criticism at times. Perhaps this is the lack of genetic mirroring showing itself. I had been considering this as a challenge now for a little over a week, and here I was suggesting it to a local charity! If I'm not careful here, I might actually have to do this ...

Date: Tuesday 22nd October 2013 – 12.18pm

"To: Andy Wallis

From: Kate

Subject: Re. Re: 5k a day (At Least)

"Hi Andy Wow, that's a great idea, and thank you as always, for your support. Your proposal definitely has legs. . . (Sorry, couldn't resist that, I can hear you groaning from here!) It's something that we can push with lots of corporate and community supporters for sure.

I think that this could really take off, the more I think about it, the more I love the idea but we should probably have a chat, let me know when will be good for you.

All the best and once again thanks for a brilliant idea!

Kate"

Of course they thought it was a "brilliant idea" and that it "could really take off" so did I. My problem was, I thought it was starting to sound like a brilliant idea for someone else to do.

I knew of a couple of challenges local to me that were similar, but this would be different. The others had a distance target in mind so their challenges didn't require them to run every day. I, on the other hand, was suggesting that I run daily and didn't care about the final distance.

The issue I had with a set distance is the same dispute I seem to have with all deadlines, time.

If I were to try and run, let's say, a thousand miles in a year, I would have two hundred miles left to do in the final week. I'm not saying that for dramatic effect, I'm serious.

In the week leading up to my email to Kate, my brain was busy sending me notes about how it might be nice to do something worthwhile for a charity, the hospice seemed the obvious choice.

My efforts were always well received but donating time to take photos for them always felt as if I was cheating somewhat, as if I wasn't really putting myself out much. That didn't sit right with me and I had to correct it somehow. Oh god, that self-esteem eh?

One of the notes Brian the brain forwarded to me had *'full* marathon' written on it, And as I had run a half marathon poorly once and was hoping to complete another as part of the challenge, I wasn't going to entertain the full 26.2 miles of hell. Besides, everyone runs marathons for charity these days, I wanted to do something that would inspire people to give their hard-earned cash to.

"Do you know how many miles you have to be running a week to get fit for that sort of thing?" I asked Brian. "Yes, that's correct, about fifty, life's too short for that" It always conjures up images of women athletes' pooing in the street anyway. No, that's not for me.

I told everyone I knew about my new idea, and most people were very encouraging and said they would support me. However, there was one person I worked with who told me that I was an "Effing idiot" for attempting it. He went on to say that I wouldn't last a month.

"Right", I thought, "You just bloody watch me".

January. It all started well. It was cold and wet, of course it was. I'd sorted out a 5k route from the hospice building, to a cinema complex in Nottingham that just happened to be working with them that year.

When I arrived at the end of the run, I was met by the manager of the complex and I had a photo taken with her, whilst holding a sign saying "1 down 364 to go". As the days went on, I ran every day. Always recording my runs in an app and posting on Facebook showing proof of the route I took, just in case people thought I might be cheating by adding the data while sitting on the sofa. Occasionally though, and annoyingly, the app didn't always record the run. When that happened, instead of adding the route manually, I just went out and did it all again. It had to be authentic. I know, idiot. My workmate was correct.

As April arrived, I started to get some pain in my legs. I could still just about run, although it was at a slower pace. The problem was I couldn't walk very far. Five-minutes was all I could manage before I had to stop or sit down. I had to get some physio or I would have to stop the challenge. The first session was hard work and painful.

151

I emerged from the clinic limping and sweating more than if I had been for a run! I was told off for not looking after myself properly too. It was stretching, proper warm-ups, and ice baths for me, daily. Eventually, I got bored of all that, my legs were improving and so just got on with running.

I ran whenever I could fit it in, but it was usually after I returned home from work. Other times I would go out at 11.30pm and complete the 5k distance. Then I'd wait for midnight to tick around, and run 5k home. This meant that I didn't have to run again that day and it felt like a day off, even though I had actually covered 10k.

I guess it's fair to say I went all out with this esteem-building, people-pleasing charity challenge. I was in all the local newspapers and on the local BBC radio and TV. My social media accounts were full with challenge updates, I was everywhere.

September came and I ran the Nottingham half marathon as part of the challenge, just as I had promised. Plus, I did manage to complete the course in one hour and fifty-six minutes, it felt so easy too. By the end of the challenge the following year, I had raised over £6,000 for the charity. I was so happy to be able to finally stop.

Before I started the running challenge, I was living with a partner and our three-year-old boy. But when I finished I was single again and living with my parents. All that working, the businesses, and running I'd been doing had put a huge amount of pressure on the relationship and I made some terrible mistakes emotionally. I wasn't at home very often and when I was, we were barely speaking. We really didn't like each other at this point and I know this was down to me. Keeping myself so busy was my way of pushing her away at the time. Of course, now I see it for what it was, attachment issues. But it has taken me ten years to come to that conclusion.

I made some deplorable choices back then, and even now, every time I pick up my son for the weekend it all comes back to me. Often just briefly, but it's there nonetheless. I hope that one day I can forgive myself for those mistakes and all the pain and heartache that myself and Brian have caused in all my relationships over the years. Right now though. Forgiveness and acceptance, seem miles away.

On his marks: Andy Wallis warms up for the challenge.

Andy's off on year-long run marathon for hospice

I Need To Know - *Part Three*

… "Well" she said, "Your birth Mum".
Mistaking this for a question I said "Yes please my
birth Mother …" As I tried to continue, she cut me
off mid-sentence.

"We've found her".

Before, I was slowly pacing up and down as people
do when standing on the phone. Now, I was quickly
darting left and right, not quite knowing what to do
with myself. I ended up leaning against the wall in
the far corner of the massive workshop at work by
the fire exit, staring at the floor.

"What? But we haven't agreed on anything", I said,
"I mean, Wow, erm. Can you tell me how much it's
going to be? " I continued. "It won't cost you a
penny," she said. "We have decided to pick three

cases from our database and do the searches for free as a Christmas gift, from us to you". I was silent, trying to take it all in as best I could. "Also, I've spoken to her and she is happy to speak with you". She said, "If you agree, she has asked that I pass her number on".

Wow, that was easy! One message and it's done.

Intermission

I've just had to get away from the laptop, I've sat and written a thousand words in this section so far today and I need a break. On the walk to Tesco to buy milk, an unusual emotional moment came over me. I needed to compose myself before I entered the shop. How strange. Sort of happy, then sad all at the same time. All these years on and my past still has a grip on me.

End of Intermission

That evening I spoke with my then-wife and my parents about the day's events. Everyone seemed thrilled that I'd gotten this far. The question of how I was feeling about it came up a lot, and also the advice that I shouldn't feel obliged to make the call if I wasn't ready. How did I feel? The truth is, I didn't know. I was confused, conflicted, and excited, I knew that much.

I am as confused and conflicted now, as I was then about the whole 'Birth Mother' subject. I mean, when all is said and done, I was relinquished by her at birth, so what right does she have to hear anything from me? No thanks to her, I turned out ok, or so I thought at the time. I didn't hear much from Brian back then, nothing I felt I could blame him for at least. But then again, I do deserve some answers to the questions that probably hadn't even formed yet. Fuck this, I'm doing it. The next day the woman from Searchline called again, and a telephone call was set up for that evening to my birth mother. Oh shit, what had I done?

Work went by that day, and I barely noticed its passing, choosing to focus mainly on the evening's call. My wife was going out that evening with our son to her Mum's so I had the house to myself which was fine by me. I was concerned it might go badly and I didn't want to look stupid in front of people.

9 pm found me standing in the lounge at home (I couldn't possibly sit down at a time like this!) I made the call. My heart was in my mouth. What the hell was I going to say? It rang for way too long ... Come on ... come on.

A click, and a man answered "Hullo?" I responded with a "Hello", a bit surprised a man's voice was on the other end of the telephone. Before I could explain the reason for my call I heard the next phrase, I remember it word for word as if it's branded into my memory.

"We know who you are and what you want, but you can piss off. I'm sorry but we are not interested…. Alright?" barked the man.

"Oh erm, ok" I managed to respond just before the phone line went dead.

Oh my god. What was that all about? I was not expecting that at all. I sunk myself into the sofa, tossed my phone onto the cushion next to me, and stared at it in disbelief. For fifteen-minutes I sat there not being able to move or think or utter a word to the empty house around me. I was just coming around a little still trying to figure out what just happened, when the phone rang. I answered, expecting it to be my wife or dad asking how it had gone …

"Andrew, is that Andrew?" "Yes, this is Andrew," I replied. "Oh hello, it's [Insert birth mother's name here] I'm so sorry about that, it's difficult you know," she said. Yes, I thought, it *is* bloody difficult! "We didn't know what to do," she continued. "Yes, it's not exactly been straightforward around here either, but I wasn't the one telling myself to piss off was I?" I wanted to say but didn't. I recall only five things from that fifteen-minute phone call;

1. I was hurt by the initial piss off vibe.
2. She firmly believed I was born ten days earlier than my recorded birth date.
3. She said I sounded like my 'dad'.
4. She said she sometimes sees my 'dad' around and he has two children.
5. She sounded very uneducated.

It's funny that I can remember the minutiae of the events pre and post-the conversation, but hardly anything of the call itself.

Also, the mention of me "sounding like my 'dad'(It's not capitalised on purpose I might add) and him having kids was put across to me as if it was a comment on the weather! Did she not realise that this now meant I had other siblings? And not to mention, her seeing my 'dad' around! That man doesn't even turn up on my birth certificate, but he's wandering around like a proper human all this time. A small part of me hoped he was dead, but no, he's been spared and allowed to have more kids. At least he kept them I suppose.

She said that it would be nice if we could speak again and if I agreed, she would leave it to me to get in touch. I deleted the number and I never did. The whole event left me with a nasty taste in my mouth. I was annoyed, I felt cheated and not considered, at the time of my birth and then again in 2003 and I had no intention of following any of that up.

As you can imagine, with the wind knocked out of me I chose not to pursue any more searches and thought I'd put it behind me and just get on with now, and stop torturing myself by looking back. Onwards and upwards Wally!

2012 now and a Facebook message that took me completely by surprise said,

"Does the name David Charles Rice mean anything to you?"

The Experiment

October 2019 and I'd just walked away from an eighteen-month relationship that had completely consumed me. I did my usual thing of shutting down and after about a week of this, she left me. And so I mourned and lamented for too long. Every day was a struggle and I ached to get her back.

So there I was, a new boy, on my own in a new town with a relatively new job and no friends. To say it was mentally tough was an understatement. I had to get my shit together, and in desperation to find any sort of social life, I took myself out into Grantham town one Friday night. Grantham is not exactly party central but I went out anyway, and it's safe to say I was pretty nervous. I trawled the pubs which were full of revellers all out in groups of mates, I had a beer in each with no idea how to even get talking to people, I mean how are you supposed to do it?

"Hi, yes I'm out on my own" "No no, I'm not a weirdo or a murderer, can I join you?"

I eventually ended up in a bar called The Nobody Inn, and after a whole evening of my lonely pub crawl, I finally somehow ended up in a big group of long-standing mates who all seemed to have been to school together. They were all about ten years younger than me and welcomed me in for the night. Now, I forced myself out that night to break the depressive and somewhat antisocial spiral I found myself in, and to my surprise it seemed to be bearing fruit. The group shared nicknames, inside jokes, stories of past trips, and nights out they had shared. For a while, they were filling me in on the background that I'd obviously not been around for, but as the night drew on that had tapered off, and I started to feel more alone than ever.

At around 2 am on Saturday morning Brian started to stir. I was about to leave to walk home, as I was feeling as if I'd outstayed my welcome and Brian wholeheartedly agreed. I was invited to someone's house as the group was all going that way. So rather than make my way home, and against Brian's better judgement, I agreed to tag along.

There were around twenty people in the house, there was food and more drinks and alongside all this, I was treated to a big plate of suspicious looks and questions like "So, who are you again?" and "How do you know these guys?" Of course, I was a nobody from the Nobody Inn as far as they were concerned and I didn't know them at all. I eventually stood up and left without saying anything to anyone because by this time I was being ignored anyway, I may as well have had a lampshade over my head.

Going out that night was an experiment, something positive to change my outlook and perspective, but in the end, I arrived home feeling more alone and isolated than before. I've not felt the need to repeat this.

Lockdown Day

On Tuesday the 24th of March 2020, sixty-seven million people woke to a whole new way of life as the first Covid-19 lockdown began in the UK.

Working and schooling from home became the norm for the vast majority, and no doubt relationships all over the UK were put under some quite considerable strain. Because I work in the food industry I was considered a Key-Worker, so I continued more or less as normal. But for someone already feeling isolated socially, being forced by law to stay at home was the last thing I needed.

I had already started a period of self-isolation due to having a temperature and cold symptoms. There was no way of testing at that time, so it was recommended

I leave work and not return for nine days. I had no idea if my symptoms were related to Covid-19, but everyone was on high alert back then and could sense a runny nose or a slight cough in someone at ten paces. For some, ten paces was still too close. I remember waking up that particular morning feeling that this was a very strange day and feeling its significance, I grabbed a notebook and pen and tried to scribble down my thoughts.

Tuesday the 24th of March 2020

It's like an old-time Christmas Day, like when I was a kid, no traffic noises, very few people outside. Except it's March and there are no kids on the street listening to brand new Sony Walkmans while testing out their new roller skates, or bikes they got from Santa. Even the clouds and the wind have stayed in today. I can usually hear traffic on the A1 that runs not far from my house, but today it is silent. I woke up at 7:30 am, came downstairs, made a coffee, opened the lounge windows wide and drew back the blinds. I never do that.

Maybe I just want to let the world in as much as I can today, if I'm not allowed to go to it, the world can come to me. Even my hectic mind is quiet today, the cognitive excavators are all parked up as if abandoned mid-scoop, adding to the serene feeling I'm sitting waist-deep in.

I lifted the classical guitar from its hanger on the wall and played something quiet in a minor key.

Was everyone feeling the same today? Locked away and kind of numb, with probably no clue as to what to do with themselves or the children. I went over to the open window in the lounge and as I did so, my neighbour left her house to go to work. We actually spoke, we never speak. She's still not happy with me after I blocked her driveway while I was fixing a car. She had to walk twenty metres from the other side of our Cul-de-sac to get to her door but you'd have thought I'd pissed on her favourite shoes!

"Are you self-isolating?" she asked, "Yes" I said "I came home from work the other day with a high temperature, to be honest, I'm pretty much over it." "I don't think it was the virus," I said with a shrug. "Well, if you need anything, just shout, " she said. "Thanks, I will." She said she would go to work as she hadn't yet been told not to (I've no idea what she does, or where she works).

I keep looking at my son's birthday present. In two days he will be eighteen and I won't be able to see him now. I was looking forward to buying him his first legal beer, but that's not going to happen as we can't venture out, even if we could, the pubs are all closed down anyway.

Just received a text from the NHS telling me to "Stay at Home" and that I should expect more advice on my condition. I'm not even sure I have a 'condition', well nothing that they can help with via text message anyway.

The loudest noise around me, even with me letting the world into my lounge through the open windows, is the central heating pipework expanding and contracting in the walls of the house.

Yes, open windows and the heating on, tut, tut! That is until I hear someone fire up an electric lawn mower, "Don't ruin the atmos' Richie!" I can hear Eddie Hitler (Ade Edmonson's character from Bottom) say in my head.

More neighbours pull up on their drive and start unloading shopping bags. It's 8:30 am I was under the impression that between 8 and 9 am was reserved for the elderly and vulnerable to shop in safety. These are the selfish neighbours at number eight, I'm at number five. My neighbour at number seven told me of late-night rows, loud music and TV so had taken a dislike to the couple. "And he's a policeman," she always tells me. Guilty as I am of judging a book by its cover, or second-hand blurb in this case, I too dislike them. Solidarity sister!

An older lady walks past now, in tight black exercise clothing and huge sunglasses that almost cover her entire head. She has cropped highlighted hair the way older but young-hearted people seem to go for these days. She must be around eighty. When I was a kid, eighty-year-old ladies would have settled for a blue rinse in tight curls and be kitted out in fur-lined, zip-up ankle boots and a pastel-coloured raincoat

I was planning to expand on my notes from that day because they ended so abruptly, but that wouldn't be true to the day as I saw it, and my thoughts at the time. So I'll just leave it at pastel-coloured raincoat.

I don't know why I'm sharing this in a book about adoption trauma. I guess it's because it's during this time that my anxiety and depression issues really became obvious, as I'm sure they did for a lot of people. We singletons spent a long time alone in our own heads and for me, that was not a great place to be.

Grief Works It's Dark Magic

Although I can fully understand why adoptees have a need to connect with their birth parents, I don't feel that need. I obviously did at one point, but not anymore.

As I scroll through the posts on the 'Adopted in the UK' Facebook page, it is full of adoptees desperately looking for birth families and I think it is fantastic that people are going to great lengths to find their families. But that just confuses me. Why don't I feel the urge to find and connect with more of my birth family?

Over a thirteen-year period I was able to gain access to my birth certificate and adoption records, as well as having a very disappointing telephone conversation with my birth mother. All the information that seemed to have satisfied my 'lost adoptee brain' was hidden in my birth records and one phone call. Doesn't seem like a lot does it?

My birth mother only knew me for a few days before giving me up. We had very little in the way of quality mother/son bonding, if any I suppose. For me, I feel there is nothing to gain from exploring this more.

How much information is enough? Would knowing about her life growing up or her life after she relinquished me really offer me anything? From where I sit today I'm saying no, I doubt it.

Being adopted has affected my mental state, of which I am certain, but I feel no kinship with my origins anymore. 'David' is not me, 'David' is gone, Andrew just carries the grief of that loss. I think.

Maybe it's the grief of that loss that drives people to want to know more and make connections with their primary life-givers.

It's well documented that grief is a big part of the psychology of the adoptee. So why is that?

Grief works it's dark magic on us in stages. These stages make up what's known as 'The Grief Cycle'. Is anyone imagining an old man crying into the handlebars or a rusty old bicycle?

Grief is something that can complete its cycle in a relatively obvious time frame, which might be a couple of years or months. Hell, it might just be weeks or days. In adoptees, however, I feel it's slowly happening over the entire adoptee's life. Now, I'm not clinically trained, but in my own opinion, I'm going to see if I can make the cycle fit.

The five stages of this hard-to-ride 'bicycle' are described thus: Denial, Anger, Depression, Bargaining, and Acceptance.

At times denial is quoted twice in the cycle, taking the place of Bargaining, but let's stick with it as it is.

Denial

I can definitely see that if you lose a loved one in later life, going through a period of denial is obvious. "If I'd just been to see them more". "Should I have suggested they see a doctor?" "What could I have done differently to keep them alive?" "Shit, are they really dead?"

But where and how does denial fit with adoptees?

Perhaps this is the newborn going into shock after being taken from her mother so early on. The panic of forced solitude. The disbelief that the warmth, sounds, and smells that baby craves are gone, and gone forever. The denial is just our mind's everlasting insecurity and lack of trust for the world we were thrown into.

Anger

Hostility and anger in varying degrees is a common theme for adoptees, and it usually comes out in later childhood and adolescence. I read lots of accounts of people claiming to be very angry as kids, causing all sorts of issues for them and their adoptive parents. I had a good friend who lived close to me growing up, he too was adopted and boy was he angry. He was forever in trouble with school, the police, his parents, and getting into the wrong crowds. He was the epitome of delinquency.

My parents were always very weary of him spending time with me. But strangely he was a great mate and always treated me and my parents with the greatest respect. If anger lies within me, it's very deep and must manifest itself in ways I've yet to appreciate. But paint me into a corner, I'll kick you in the balls.

Depression.

Stage three of the cycle. I have suffered from depressive periods in varying degrees for about ten years now. It leaves me feeling as if I'm standing on an abandoned beach, it is cold and desolate, and I'm alone. Could this possibly be part of my perpetual grief?

I've always been lucky enough to have a full-time job but was never fully satisfied with it. Always feeling I was destined for more. Depressive thoughts started, then Brian the brain started to look ever more deeply for things to occupy 'us'. I can never place where my depression comes from but it takes hold nonetheless. Thankfully now I'm finding ways to cope and I see these moments coming from a mile away. I'm not saying I have all the answers here, but I'm learning.

Bargaining

This could also be seen as guilt, after a loss people resort to the same sort of questions they had right at the start during the denial process, "If only I'd …" but what if I'd …" and perhaps adoptees who start their journey to trace original parentage go through a similar process, "Was I not a good baby?" "Did I cry too much?" "Why was I not wanted?". This is where I struggle because I don't have these questions within. I'm not suggesting they are not present in others, just that I can't find them in me, yet.

Acceptance

The mental Health Charity 'Mind' on their website, quotes acceptance in this way:

"Acceptance does not mean that somebody likes the situation or that it is right or fair, but rather it involves acknowledging the implications of the loss and the new circumstances and being prepared to move forward in a new direction."

In my opinion, acceptance happens later on in an adoptee's life, middle age in fact. Why else are there so many forty-something adoptees finally coming out of the 'fog' of adoption? Once the situation of relinquishment has been accepted we can then look for ways to heal. Through for example; counselling, reading, joining Facebook groups, or as I am doing writing about my experiences to aid catharsis. In whatever way we choose to carry this part out, and there are a lot more ways than just the few I've mentioned, it seems to me to be preparing to move forward in a new direction.

We are looking for solidarity, for answers in others. And after a lifelong battle with unrecognised grief, and all that healing we do in later life, we are gaining acceptance. Then, we can think about connecting with birth parents, and we do, in our thousands.

I do consider the possibility that, if and when I have gained enough acceptance, I too will need to connect with my roots. But by then it could be all too late.

Interview With The Daily Telegraph.

Back in 2005, I was interviewed by a journalist from The Daily Telegraph. I was asked by the people at Searchine if they could pass on my contact details to the newspaper. The article was entitled 'It's a Life Sentence With No Reprieve' and in a roundabout way, it asked questions about the closed adoption system. The lead story concerned a couple in South London who, in 2000 had their four children taken from them, two were fostered out while the other two were adopted elsewhere.

A court had held them responsible for poisoning one of the children with prescription drugs. The sixteen-month-old had swallowed "twelve to sixteen" pills, prescribed for the eldest child to reduce bedwetting. However, the toxicology reports said that "less than one of the pills could have killed a child under five".

It is not made clear in the article where the blame lay or what the outcome was, choosing rather to focus on the unfairness and grief the couple had experienced owing to the loss of their family.

Amongst the various people interviewed, from birth parents to adoptees, my little thirty-one-year-old face appears above a column of words formed from the interview I had over the phone.

I've kept the newspaper in my adoption folder all these years, here are those words …

"My birth mother gave me up for adoption because she was twenty and didn't have space in her life for a child. My adopters were always very upfront about the circumstances and I couldn't have asked for a better childhood with them.

Nevertheless, seven years ago, when I was in my mid-twenties, I wanted to find my birth mother.

You can't always put your finger on it, but something is always a miss, you feel there is a hole that is never going to get filled.

Back in 1999, my adoptive parents were happy when I found my birth certificate with my birth mother's name on it. They weren't so sure this year when I rang an agency 'Searchline' that was able to give me her telephone number. My adoptive mother said she was worried that I would disappear and that she would be forgotten, although I was able to reassure her that I would never do that.

When I made the call I was geared up for feeling over the moon, but it wasn't like that. My birth mother sounded quite flat and unemotional. She didn't even remember my birthday correctly. She said I sounded like my 'dad', whom I have never been interested in finding.

Open adoptions could feel more like permanent fostering and could be quite difficult for the adopters who might feel they had to fight to keep the child.

I have heard it said that you can't have too many people love a child and although an extended family is good, when it is extended from adoptive to birth families, it could become very confusing for all concerned."

I don't want to comment too much on the story of the couple specifically, but it does raise some interesting ideas for me.

From what I know about my relinquishment, I was given up, not forcibly removed from my birth mother. But so many adoptees were placed with new families to keep them safe. This has to cause trauma. How does a person adopted in this way begin to process that information? Are they grateful for essentially being saved? I would estimate that yes, there must be an element of salvation for them.

But then to be removed rather than given up? In the case of the family in the article, there seemed to be an argument for a miscarriage of justice, were they innocent, was this just an accident? Or had something more sinister transpired?

How does the child begin to place the emotions they must be left with after such a traumatic start? Is there relief for being potentially 'saved'? Grief at the loss of the parents because it could all have been an innocent mistake? Anger that the birth parents allowed this to happen or at the justice system for misjudging the case and stealing a normal life from the child? Is there perhaps shame that it happened at all?

Have I just described the thoughts and emotions of all adoptees, regardless of their beginnings? Perhaps yes.

I have no issues with talking to others about my experience of adoption, as mine was relatively uneventful by comparison to some, and by all accounts, pretty straightforward. Yet the relinquishment has affected me, and in some quite dramatic and negative ways. I truly hope that adult adoptees who started their lives in incomprehensible ways can recognise it and find a way of gaining peace.

After reading my thoughts in this article from twenty years ago it's indisputable that I had some understanding that I was different and the loss certainly wasn't alien to me even then. I also noted that my parents' feelings seemed to be almost more important to me than my own. I was very conscious of not hurting them during my search for my birth family and I wonder how much of an influence that was on my decision to not continue my search.

I think I still stand by my suggestion that open adoptions could be confusing for the families and the children involved. I would think that they need to be handled very carefully if good mental health for all concerned is to be maintained.

My final thought is not quite so serious. In the photo of me, I had this tiny little gappy beard going on. Why didn't someone just pull me to one side and say "Andy, Mate. Give it up. There is a time and a place for facial hair on you and now isn't it … OK?".

I Need To Know - *The Conclusion*

Right, where were we?

… Jumping forward to 2012 now and a Facebook message that took me completely by surprise said,

"Does the name David Charles Rice mean anything to you?"

This message found my Facebook inbox while I was sitting at my dining table one Friday evening. For the life of me, I can't recall when during the year it was. I know it wasn't summer, it was too cold. "Oh my god!" I said out loud, completely shocked. My then partner (Yes, another one, probably all credit for that goes to Brian, again!) said "What?" "I've just had a Facebook message from someone, who is not on my friends list, and knows my birth name!" I squeaked. "Oh!?" she said, "Let's see?" "Should I reply?" I asked. "Sounds like it could be a scam," she said.

That did cross my mind to be fair, I thought some more. "Nobody outside of this family knows that Andy Wallis was David Rice, do they?" I said. "Sod this, I'm going to reply".

I sent back four words "Yes. That was me"

I nervously waited. Within a few minutes, a reply pinged back. Ok so, apologies here, but this is all I can recall, so I'm not going to waste your valuable time making up stuff.

So, who was the person who was looking for 'David'?

My sister. Yes, before I was conceived by my birth mother and the invisible man, she had two other children adopted. Both girls, with the eldest being three years my senior. Yes, I know, I have been holding on to this information until I could write it here, I'm sorry. Do you feel a bit cheated? Oh well, let's move on, it's done now.

Of course, I already knew I had two half-sisters because I was the youngest and so they were included in my records.

Sarah being the middle child, had details of our older sister, but not me, for obvious reasons. So how did she find me?

Stop. Just a second here.

I've recently had lunch with Sarah and she was pleased that I had included her in the book, but Jokingly complained about being called 'Sarah'. Instead she wanted to be called 'Anne'. So here you go 'Anne', consider it done.

If you recall, I placed a message on the Searchline website back in 2003. That included our birth mother's name in full. When Anne used that name on the ever-expanding internet, what should pop up but that message from me nearly ten years previous. Can you imagine finding out you had a brother all this time from a search like that?

Anne said she started looking for Andy Wallis on Facebook and messaged all the Andys that returned during her search. After a couple of No's she tried me, and jackpot! There I was. Early on in my search, I thought it would be easier to find birth mum first. Then of course I hung up the old deer-stalker hat following the very disappointing phone call with her, so I hadn't tried looking for either of my sisters.

She still lived in the Derbyshire area and I was in Nottingham. We were both so excited about the prospect of her finding me, therefore we agreed to meet at 11 am at a Starbucks coffee house the next day. We chose one as close to the middle as we could find. My partner wasn't happy about me doing this so early on after first contact but I was determined, so went along anyway.

I wasn't nervous as I travelled the eight miles to Starbucks. However, as soon as I encroached on the car park the nerves kicked in. The telephone conversation I had with my birth mother all those years ago went round and round in my head. What if my partner was right? What if this was a bad idea? Could I take to being let down again? I didn't know who this Anne was, she could be anyone. I could have a pillowcase over my head, thrown in a van, and be in a shop window in Amsterdam, wearing a leather thong by the following day. I shook myself right. It's all going to be fine, plus you're not bad-looking but you're no Brad Pitt, Wally, nobody is going to want to pay to see you do that, you idiot.

I arrived at the shop first. Or so I thought, Anne was sitting in the car with her husband, waiting. She told me she saw me go in and knowing it was me, followed on. We didn't look much alike but our eyes looked similar, it was pretty clear that we were half-siblings, neither of us were surprised. We sat, drank coffee, and chatted, nervously to start with, but we soon settled. I took my adoption records, just in case, but we didn't look at them. It sounded like she had had a happy life with her adopted family and I reported the same for me. Anne said she hadn't spoken to our birth mother but planned to. I told her my phone call story and said I didn't feel like I could pursue it. Over the next hour, we filled each other in on the key points of our separate lives and promised to keep in touch as we parted.

I couldn't drive home afterward, I was full of nervous excitement so I walked around the Ikea store that was close by. I needed something to calm me down and nothing knocks the wind out of your sails like being dragged along on the tide of Saturday shoppers with yellow and blue bags full of tea lights, does it?

For a good while Anne and I, true to our word, kept in touch.

We started to buy each other childlike gifts for birthdays as we had missed so many. I remember one year I bought her Kerplunk. You know the straws and marbles game from the 1970s. I received a Matchbox car and a Beano comic. I have the comic framed on my kitchen wall.

Anne did meet up with our mum in the end, but I still haven't. She told me that she lies. She puts this down to the fact that she's spent so much of her life covering up her past that she doesn't know what's true and what isn't anymore. I can understand that, I guess. Our birth mum is married, but not to the man she was originally, and she has had two boys. They must be in their forties now. They have both given her grandchildren. I'm glad, at least for her, after the very difficult three years of pregnancy and relinquishment, she has been able to create a family of her own after all.

A few years ago, Anne asked if I wanted to meet our birth mum then she would facilitate it for me. I thought about it for a long time and then agreed. In the end, I bottled it and didn't go. It's not right for me. I've got my parents. I don't need any more.

She also found Jane the eldest sibling, she passed on her details to me and we were able to meet. I found her hard work, we haven't met again. You know when you just don't 'gel' with someone? She and I definitely share a family resemblance, and that was nice to see, but I felt nothing towards her, not in the way I do when I think of Anne.

Unfortunately, like me, Anne suffers from depression and anxiety issues, but hers are often quite debilitating, so we often lose touch as she and I both cut the other out, it's not personal, and we both understand that, as we've been chopping people off our Christmas card list all our adult lives.

After the journey that started for me in 1998, I now have a little bit of closure, I know more about my birth mum, through Anne, and I have two sisters, two brothers, and two siblings I know nothing about. As well as nieces and nephews, two of whom I have met and they are both lovely.

Oh, one more thing… Yes, in a Colombo way!

Anne told me recently that when I was born her adoptive mum was given the chance to adopt me too. This was shocking to hear. And we were both a little saddened by it. Her mum had to decline as she didn't feel that she was financially able to take on another child. We had two chances to grow up together but sadly still lived apart for all these years.

A Not So Found Poem

Flicking through my adoption file in its old green A4 ring binder folder (which I realise is older than my twenty-two-year-old son!) Come to think of it, I have shirts older than him too. Well, now I'm just thinking about other stuff that is older than him …
Oh that big saucepan and that hammer I acquired from Dad, erm? … The cheese grater, ah yes, I love that cheese grater! Anyway ...

In the folder, at the back, I stored about thirty sheets of notepaper. Only the first sheet had any notes on it. I snapped the rings open and removed them for recycling, but something stopped me.

"I'll just look through it to make sure I haven't noted anything further back" I thought. I do tend to write from the back of notebooks if I need to be able to find that information quickly. There was nothing, old, yellowing, and blank, but enough about me. Then I spotted something just before the last page, six lines of minimal, neat, and flowing handwriting, not mine, and from nobody, I can recall writing this way.

Where the hell did this come from?

This folder is as personal as it gets to me and only a handful of people have ever been shown it. I can only assume that this had been written by someone before I had the note paper. Was this note paper second hand to me? Who buys second-hand note paper, and in individual leaves?! Ok, so that's got *me* written all over it, to be honest.

The words written on the page appear to be almost a poem from a broken heart. Was this an ex-girlfriend who just couldn't contain the grief of the ending of our relationship? To be truthful, this has *me* written all over it too. My life is littered with past romances thanks to my adoption, and Brian no doubt.

After a bit of internet digging, it's not from one of my ex-girlfriends, no, it's song lyrics by the 1990s band Roxette. The song is called 'Fading like a Flower (Every time you leave)' and was released in 1991, from the album Joyride. Mystery sort of solved eh? But it doesn't explain why it was written in my folder or by whom. So it's still a little intriguing, just not as exciting. Now I'm a bit disappointed.

The words aren't laid out as a poem, just written across each line, filling the top of the page with the inclusion of the odd comma.

I've managed to pick through the 'poem' and I think I've managed to read it all correctly as some of the lettering is entirely illegible.

Why am I sharing this with you? The words resonate with me and my little attachment disorder and the subsequent numbness I feel being in relationships over the years. This handy little 'Bolt on' inside Brian causes me to fade like a flower, and run away. "Every time you leave the room" - Please don't leave me. Come back. I wonder if she will come back.

There goes my heart turning to stone again,
Right on bloody cue! Thanks Brian!

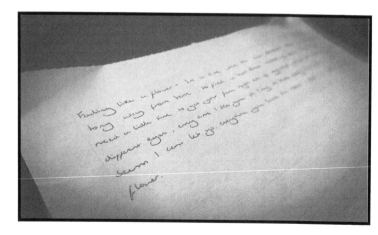

The Lid Is Off

When I had the idea to write about my adoption for the book, I was expecting to end up struggling with enough detail to make even one chapter out of it. But I soon realised that it was bigger than that. The memories I thought I'd lost forever just came from nowhere and they just grew and grew. I can highly recommend the power of writing, it really has been amazing to me.

Some writers say that the writing started for them after a difficult time and after gaining clarity had an urge to write. The process of writing came from a very confusing and depressing time for me. I was still in that funk when I chose to write, and eagle-eyed readers may see that in my finished articles on the blog. As the words hit the screen and over time you will notice my writing voice has been elevated bit by bit. Now I'm writing with a little humour here and there and finding more light in what is, let's face it, a dark and depressing subject at times. What's that called? Gallows humour, that's it.

Some of this is down to the process, I'm sure. A lot of it though, is down to finding the adoptee community, and then, even more amazing to me is the fact that I've found an audience. I never in my wildest dreams imagined that the ramblings of a miserable fifty-year-old would be of any interest to anyone but that miserable fifty-year-old. So to those people, I say thank you. Now my writing is for me and that community. It's for us. I'm really hoping that this book and the Who's Wally? blog might, in some small way, help one or two other people to have their moment of clarity, because writing this and reading others' work has certainly helped me.

I've thought long and hard about the final chapter because I can't round it all off with a happy walk off into the sunset, as that would suggest I'm at the finish and all is well, wouldn't it?

If you've got to this point in the book then it means one of two things;

1. You've read the entire book
2. You don't own the book but have just picked it up, and read the last chapter, so you can ruin it for someone else … Shame on you I say … Shame!

Hopefully, it's the first one, and you have probably realised this book has asked more than it has answered. I don't have the answers, but when I started writing, I didn't have the questions either. I was writing myself out of depression, mainly because I felt I had no other option. On the Who's Wally? blog **(www.whoswally.co.uk)** I've likened my cognitive self to a jigsaw puzzle. For so many years the lid of the box had never been removed, I could hear the puzzle pieces moving about inside, but that was all. Now, after a few months of collating my thoughts, feelings, and emotions together, the lid of the box is off and I can see the pieces. I might even have the start of the edges assembled.

Going from someone who has been wandering around in the adoption fog, completely oblivious of its effect on his life. To someone now with a clear understanding of the issues being faced, is incredible.

Through interactions on social media, reading fellow adoptees' books and blogs, writing for myself, guest writing for others, as well as being invited to speak on adoptee podcasts, I'm really starting to feel part of a worldwide community of people who all seem to be dealing with the same idiosyncrasies. And here I was thinking I was alone.

The answers aren't coming easily, but I'm on the right path to be able to find them. If you are coming from the second point in my little list above, then I'm afraid there is no Whodunit? to be gleaned here, so nerr!

"Never mind all this waffle, come on, who actually *is* Wally?" - Damn it! I knew you were going to ask me that!

I'm still unsure but I know one thing, he's not the thin guy with the glasses and red and white bobble hat, no matter how many times Google tries to tell me otherwise! I've got to admit on the odd occasion, Ok every week, for months! (Don't judge me!) I've been opening an Incognito search page and typing "whos wally" just to see if the blog appears anywhere near the useful search results. All I ever get back is a red hat. This is weird because I thought he was supposed to be hard to spot! One of these days I'll beat that skinny little cartoon geek to the top of the page!

Something else I know is that 'Wally' really isn't just 'Andy Wallis', he is still 'David Rice' too, and I firmly believe that blending the two of us is the key to it all. I need to stop fighting with them both and come to an agreement. I'm calling for a ceasefire, an internal amnesty if you will.

I was desperately looking for a pun there, but I can't make one work, if you could just roll your eyes as if you'd just read one … That's great, thanks.

I'm slowly coming to terms with it all, the depression, the anxiety, the attachment issues, I've looked back and seen it all happen in my past as well as tackling it in the present. In the future, I want to make it a thing of the past, that will be a present to myself (are you following this?!!).

Now, have you seen the box of flux capacitors? And where are the keys to that Delorean? It's going to be a lengthy road. "Roads? Where we're going we don't need roads!"

(Sorry, If you didn't know, all this bit is a reference to Back to the Future you didn't think I would just end it normally now did you?)

The End

No, wait. finishing with the usual *The End* feels wrong. It might be the end of the book but I'm not at the end of this journey, it seems to me that I'm only just beginning. The mental health community has adopted the semicolon to signify that what follows is related to what precedes and that a person's story is not over, just because of their mental health. I have one tattooed on my right wrist, except mine has the upper dot made into the shape of a quaver (an eighth musical note).

It helps to remind me not to trust my thoughts all the time, and that music is the one thing that seems to help me connect with my stifled emotions.

With that in mind … ♪

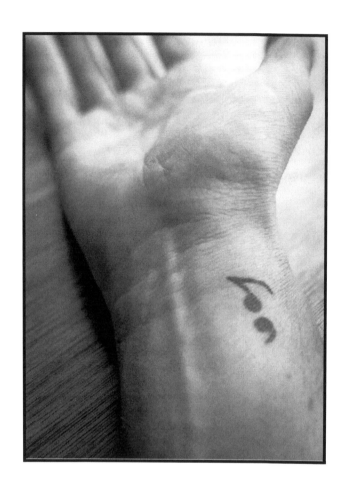

Acknowledgment of Some Lovely People

Mum and Dad

Thank you for giving little David a home and for loving me unconditionally. You have always been there for me, whatever the weather, you are amazing. I love you. Thanks also for correcting my timeline errors.

Em

Your love, patience, encouragement, and willingness to join me on this journey have been amazing. Without your persistence in the beginning, this book would never have been written. Although I've not made your life easy of late, you are still here with me and for that, I will always be grateful. I just wish I felt worthy of it all. Thank you, I love you.

Fiona Myles

Thank you for your help and encouragement as well as for being responsible for bringing me out of the adoption fog through your book 'Adoption Trauma'.

Gaynor Cherieann

Thank you for your encouragement and for helping with the book edits.

Anne Heffron

Thank you for your book 'You Don't Look Adopted' and for your kind words. Thanks also for guest blogging on the 'Who's Wally?' blog. That was very cool, and also for asking me to write for yours.

Anna Anderson

Thank you for your time and advice with the writing, for reading the drafts and giving 'Who's Wally?' such a lovely review.

Fiona Baxter

Thank you for agreeing to proofread my final draft. You consume a lot of books, so I knew if you liked it, then I was on the right track.

Anne Hall

Thank you for your advice during the early stages of my writing. You are a good egg.

Last, but by no means least, Thank you to the adoption community for your support and encouragement while I spilled my mind onto the blog. I didn't even know you all existed when I first started! You have been there for the low points as well as the highs and I appreciate you all.

You all helped so much in the production of this book and I'm extremely grateful.

Something Further For Your Eyes, Ears, and Brians.

If, after reading 'Who's Wally?' you feel you want to know more about adoption trauma or need advice on mental health, then here are some of the resources I have found helpful and interesting.

Blogs

Who's wally? - www.whoswally.co.uk

Anne Heffron - www.anneheffron.com/blog

Anne Stoneson - Labyrinth Healing - labyrinthhealing.com/blog

Tony Ingham - https://tobyingham.com/abandonment -trauma-in-adopted-adults

Books

Nancy Verrier - Coming Home to Self

Nancy Verrier - The Primal Wound

Fiona Myles - Adoption Trauma

Anne Heffron - You Don't Look Adopted

Gaynor Cherieann - An Adoptee's Journey, Letters of My Life

Fred Nicora - Forbidden Roots

Podcasts

Simon Benn - Thriving Adoptee's - www.thrivingadoptees.com

Wandering tree - wanderingtreeadoptee.com

Adoptees at work - Find it wherever you get your podcasts.

Mental Health Advice - UK

NHS - www.nhs.uk/nhs-services/mental-health-services

Mind - www.mind.org.uk

Mental Health Foundation -
www.mentalhealth.org.uk

A Kind Request

If you have enjoyed this book, It would be fantastic if you could share it with others, you never know who might benefit from reading about my mind.

Also, It would be great if you could please leave 'Who's Wally?' a review via Amazon, Goodreads, or wherever you bought this copy.

Thank you so much.

Andy

Printed in Great Britain
by Amazon